C-796   CAREER EXAMINATION SERIES

*This is your
PASSBOOK for...*

Social Work Assistant

*Test Preparation Study Guide
Questions & Answers*

COPYRIGHT NOTICE

This book is SOLELY intended for, is sold ONLY to, and its use is RESTRICTED to individual, bona fide applicants or candidates who qualify by virtue of having seriously filed applications for appropriate license, certificate, professional and/or promotional advancement, higher school matriculation, scholarship, or other legitimate requirements of education and/or governmental authorities.

This book is NOT intended for use, class instruction, tutoring, training, duplication, copying, reprinting, excerption, or adaptation, etc., by:

1) Other publishers
2) Proprietors and/or Instructors of "Coaching" and/or Preparatory Courses
3) Personnel and/or Training Divisions of commercial, industrial, and governmental organizations
4) Schools, colleges, or universities and/or their departments and staffs, including teachers and other personnel
5) Testing Agencies or Bureaus
6) Study groups which seek by the purchase of a single volume to copy and/or duplicate and/or adapt this material for use by the group as a whole without having purchased individual volumes for each of the members of the group
7) Et al.

Such persons would be in violation of appropriate Federal and State statutes.

PROVISION OF LICENSING AGREEMENTS – Recognized educational, commercial, industrial, and governmental institutions and organizations, and others legitimately engaged in educational pursuits, including training, testing, and measurement activities, may address request for a licensing agreement to the copyright owners, who will determine whether, and under what conditions, including fees and charges, the materials in this book may be used them. In other words, a licensing facility exists for the legitimate use of the material in this book on other than an individual basis. However, it is asseverated and affirmed here that the material in this book CANNOT be used without the receipt of the express permission of such a licensing agreement from the Publishers. Inquiries re licensing should be addressed to the company, attention rights and permissions department.

All rights reserved, including the right of reproduction in whole or in part, in any form or by any means, electronic or mechanical, including photocopying, recording, or by any information storage and retrieval system, without permission in writing from the Publisher.

Copyright © 2025 by
National Learning Corporation

212 Michael Drive, Syosset, NY 11791
(516) 921-8888 • www.passbooks.com
E-mail: info@passbooks.com

PASSBOOK® SERIES

THE *PASSBOOK® SERIES* has been created to prepare applicants and candidates for the ultimate academic battlefield – the examination room.

At some time in our lives, each and every one of us may be required to take an examination – for validation, matriculation, admission, qualification, registration, certification, or licensure.

Based on the assumption that every applicant or candidate has met the basic formal educational standards, has taken the required number of courses, and read the necessary texts, the *PASSBOOK® SERIES* furnishes the one special preparation which may assure passing with confidence, instead of failing with insecurity. Examination questions – together with answers – are furnished as the basic vehicle for study so that the mysteries of the examination and its compounding difficulties may be eliminated or diminished by a sure method.

This book is meant to help you pass your examination provided that you qualify and are serious in your objective.

The entire field is reviewed through the huge store of content information which is succinctly presented through a provocative and challenging approach – the question-and-answer method.

A climate of success is established by furnishing the correct answers at the end of each test.

You soon learn to recognize types of questions, forms of questions, and patterns of questioning. You may even begin to anticipate expected outcomes.

You perceive that many questions are repeated or adapted so that you can gain acute insights, which may enable you to score many sure points.

You learn how to confront new questions, or types of questions, and to attack them confidently and work out the correct answers.

You note objectives and emphases, and recognize pitfalls and dangers, so that you may make positive educational adjustments.

Moreover, you are kept fully informed in relation to new concepts, methods, practices, and directions in the field.

You discover that you are actually taking the examination all the time: you are preparing for the examination by "taking" an examination, not by reading extraneous and/or supererogatory textbooks.

In short, this PASSBOOK®, used directedly, should be an important factor in helping you to pass your test.

SOCIAL WORK ASSISTANT

DUTIES
Social Work Assistants are employed in the residential facilities and community programs of the Office of Mental Health and the Office of Mental Retardation and Developmental Disabilities, and in the residential facilities of the Office of Alcoholism and Substance Abuse Services.
As a Social Work Assistant, you would, under the supervision of professional staff, directly provide or assist in the provision of various social work activities in support of a plan of service for consumers. This could include individual assessments; identification, implementation, coordination and evaluation of services; and communication with consumers and other involved parties.

SUBJECT OF EXAMINATION
The written test will be designed to test for knowledge, skills, and/or abilities in such areas as:
1. Providing social work services to individuals with mental disabilities;
2. Interviewing;
3. Preparing written material; and
4. Understanding and interpreting written materials relating to social work practice.

HOW TO TAKE A TEST

I. YOU MUST PASS AN EXAMINATION

A. WHAT EVERY CANDIDATE SHOULD KNOW

Examination applicants often ask us for help in preparing for the written test. What can I study in advance? What kinds of questions will be asked? How will the test be given? How will the papers be graded?

As an applicant for a civil service examination, you may be wondering about some of these things. Our purpose here is to suggest effective methods of advance study and to describe civil service examinations.

Your chances for success on this examination can be increased if you know how to prepare. Those "pre-examination jitters" can be reduced if you know what to expect. You can even experience an adventure in good citizenship if you know why civil service exams are given.

B. WHY ARE CIVIL SERVICE EXAMINATIONS GIVEN?

Civil service examinations are important to you in two ways. As a citizen, you want public jobs filled by employees who know how to do their work. As a job seeker, you want a fair chance to compete for that job on an equal footing with other candidates. The best-known means of accomplishing this two-fold goal is the competitive examination.

Exams are widely publicized throughout the nation. They may be administered for jobs in federal, state, city, municipal, town or village governments or agencies.

Any citizen may apply, with some limitations, such as the age or residence of applicants. Your experience and education may be reviewed to see whether you meet the requirements for the particular examination. When these requirements exist, they are reasonable and applied consistently to all applicants. Thus, a competitive examination may cause you some uneasiness now, but it is your privilege and safeguard.

C. HOW ARE CIVIL SERVICE EXAMS DEVELOPED?

Examinations are carefully written by trained technicians who are specialists in the field known as "psychological measurement," in consultation with recognized authorities in the field of work that the test will cover. These experts recommend the subject matter areas or skills to be tested; only those knowledges or skills important to your success on the job are included. The most reliable books and source materials available are used as references. Together, the experts and technicians judge the difficulty level of the questions.

Test technicians know how to phrase questions so that the problem is clearly stated. Their ethics do not permit "trick" or "catch" questions. Questions may have been tried out on sample groups, or subjected to statistical analysis, to determine their usefulness.

Written tests are often used in combination with performance tests, ratings of training and experience, and oral interviews. All of these measures combine to form the best-known means of finding the right person for the right job.

II. HOW TO PASS THE WRITTEN TEST

A. NATURE OF THE EXAMINATION

To prepare intelligently for civil service examinations, you should know how they differ from school examinations you have taken. In school you were assigned certain definite pages to read or subjects to cover. The examination questions were quite detailed and usually emphasized memory. Civil service exams, on the other hand, try to discover your present ability to perform the duties of a position, plus your potentiality to learn these duties. In other words, a civil service exam attempts to predict how successful you will be. Questions cover such a broad area that they cannot be as minute and detailed as school exam questions.

In the public service similar kinds of work, or positions, are grouped together in one "class." This process is known as *position-classification*. All the positions in a class are paid according to the salary range for that class. One class title covers all of these positions, and they are all tested by the same examination.

B. FOUR BASIC STEPS

1) Study the announcement

How, then, can you know what subjects to study? Our best answer is: "Learn as much as possible about the class of positions for which you've applied." The exam will test the knowledge, skills and abilities needed to do the work.

Your most valuable source of information about the position you want is the official exam announcement. This announcement lists the training and experience qualifications. Check these standards and apply only if you come reasonably close to meeting them.

The brief description of the position in the examination announcement offers some clues to the subjects which will be tested. Think about the job itself. Review the duties in your mind. Can you perform them, or are there some in which you are rusty? Fill in the blank spots in your preparation.

Many jurisdictions preview the written test in the exam announcement by including a section called "Knowledge and Abilities Required," "Scope of the Examination," or some similar heading. Here you will find out specifically what fields will be tested.

2) Review your own background

Once you learn in general what the position is all about, and what you need to know to do the work, ask yourself which subjects you already know fairly well and which need improvement. You may wonder whether to concentrate on improving your strong areas or on building some background in your fields of weakness. When the announcement has specified "some knowledge" or "considerable knowledge," or has used adjectives like "beginning principles of…" or "advanced … methods," you can get a clue as to the number and difficulty of questions to be asked in any given field. More questions, and hence broader coverage, would be included for those subjects which are more important in the work. Now weigh your strengths and weaknesses against the job requirements and prepare accordingly.

3) Determine the level of the position

Another way to tell how intensively you should prepare is to understand the level of the job for which you are applying. Is it the entering level? In other words, is this the position in which beginners in a field of work are hired? Or is it an intermediate or advanced level? Sometimes this is indicated by such words as "Junior" or "Senior" in the class title. Other jurisdictions use Roman numerals to designate the level – Clerk I, Clerk II, for example. The word "Supervisor" sometimes appears in the title. If the level is not indicated by the title, check the description of duties. Will you be working under very close supervision, or will you have responsibility for independent decisions in this work?

4) Choose appropriate study materials

Now that you know the subjects to be examined and the relative amount of each subject to be covered, you can choose suitable study materials. For beginning level jobs, or even advanced ones, if you have a pronounced weakness in some aspect of your training, read a modern, standard textbook in that field. Be sure it is up to date and has general coverage. Such books are normally available at your library, and the librarian will be glad to help you locate one. For entry-level positions, questions of appropriate difficulty are chosen – neither highly advanced questions, nor those too simple. Such questions require careful thought but not advanced training.

If the position for which you are applying is technical or advanced, you will read more advanced, specialized material. If you are already familiar with the basic principles of your field, elementary textbooks would waste your time. Concentrate on advanced textbooks and technical periodicals. Think through the concepts and review difficult problems in your field.

These are all general sources. You can get more ideas on your own initiative, following these leads. For example, training manuals and publications of the government agency which employs workers in your field can be useful, particularly for technical and professional positions. A letter or visit to the government department involved may result in more specific study suggestions, and certainly will provide you with a more definite idea of the exact nature of the position you are seeking.

III. KINDS OF TESTS

Tests are used for purposes other than measuring knowledge and ability to perform specified duties. For some positions, it is equally important to test ability to make adjustments to new situations or to profit from training. In others, basic mental abilities not dependent on information are essential. Questions which test these things may not appear as pertinent to the duties of the position as those which test for knowledge and information. Yet they are often highly important parts of a fair examination. For very general questions, it is almost impossible to help you direct your study efforts. What we can do is to point out some of the more common of these general abilities needed in public service positions and describe some typical questions.

1) General information

Broad, general information has been found useful for predicting job success in some kinds of work. This is tested in a variety of ways, from vocabulary lists to questions about current events. Basic background in some field of work, such as sociology or economics, may be sampled in a group of questions. Often these are principles which have become familiar to most persons through exposure rather than through formal training. It is difficult to advise you how to study for these questions; being alert to the world around you is our best suggestion.

2) Verbal ability

An example of an ability needed in many positions is verbal or language ability. Verbal ability is, in brief, the ability to use and understand words. Vocabulary and grammar tests are typical measures of this ability. Reading comprehension or paragraph interpretation questions are common in many kinds of civil service tests. You are given a paragraph of written material and asked to find its central meaning.

3) Numerical ability

Number skills can be tested by the familiar arithmetic problem, by checking paired lists of numbers to see which are alike and which are different, or by interpreting charts and graphs. In the latter test, a graph may be printed in the test booklet which you are asked to use as the basis for answering questions.

4) Observation

A popular test for law-enforcement positions is the observation test. A picture is shown to you for several minutes, then taken away. Questions about the picture test your ability to observe both details and larger elements.

5) Following directions

In many positions in the public service, the employee must be able to carry out written instructions dependably and accurately. You may be given a chart with several columns, each column listing a variety of information. The questions require you to carry out directions involving the information given in the chart.

6) Skills and aptitudes

Performance tests effectively measure some manual skills and aptitudes. When the skill is one in which you are trained, such as typing or shorthand, you can practice. These tests are often very much like those given in business school or high school courses. For many of the other skills and aptitudes, however, no short-time preparation can be made. Skills and abilities natural to you or that you have developed throughout your lifetime are being tested.

Many of the general questions just described provide all the data needed to answer the questions and ask you to use your reasoning ability to find the answers. Your best preparation for these tests, as well as for tests of facts and ideas, is to be at your physical and mental best. You, no doubt, have your own methods of getting into an exam-taking mood and keeping "in shape." The next section lists some ideas on this subject.

IV. KINDS OF QUESTIONS

Only rarely is the "essay" question, which you answer in narrative form, used in civil service tests. Civil service tests are usually of the short-answer type. Full instructions for answering these questions will be given to you at the examination. But in case this is your first experience with short-answer questions and separate answer sheets, here is what you need to know:

1) **Multiple-choice Questions**

Most popular of the short-answer questions is the "multiple choice" or "best answer" question. It can be used, for example, to test for factual knowledge, ability to solve problems or judgment in meeting situations found at work.

A multiple-choice question is normally one of three types—
- It can begin with an incomplete statement followed by several possible endings. You are to find the one ending which *best* completes the statement, although some of the others may not be entirely wrong.
- It can also be a complete statement in the form of a question which is answered by choosing one of the statements listed.

- It can be in the form of a problem – again you select the best answer.

Here is an example of a multiple-choice question with a discussion which should give you some clues as to the method for choosing the right answer:

When an employee has a complaint about his assignment, the action which will *best* help him overcome his difficulty is to
    A. discuss his difficulty with his coworkers
    B. take the problem to the head of the organization
    C. take the problem to the person who gave him the assignment
    D. say nothing to anyone about his complaint

In answering this question, you should study each of the choices to find which is best. Consider choice "A" – Certainly an employee may discuss his complaint with fellow employees, but no change or improvement can result, and the complaint remains unresolved. Choice "B" is a poor choice since the head of the organization probably does not know what assignment you have been given, and taking your problem to him is known as "going over the head" of the supervisor. The supervisor, or person who made the assignment, is the person who can clarify it or correct any injustice. Choice "C" is, therefore, correct. To say nothing, as in choice "D," is unwise. Supervisors have and interest in knowing the problems employees are facing, and the employee is seeking a solution to his problem.

2) True/False Questions

The "true/false" or "right/wrong" form of question is sometimes used. Here a complete statement is given. Your job is to decide whether the statement is right or wrong.

SAMPLE: A roaming cell-phone call to a nearby city costs less than a non-roaming call to a distant city.

This statement is wrong, or false, since roaming calls are more expensive.

This is not a complete list of all possible question forms, although most of the others are variations of these common types. You will always get complete directions for answering questions. Be sure you understand *how* to mark your answers – ask questions until you do.

V. RECORDING YOUR ANSWERS

Computer terminals are used more and more today for many different kinds of exams.
For an examination with very few applicants, you may be told to record your answers in the test booklet itself. Separate answer sheets are much more common. If this separate answer sheet is to be scored by machine – and this is often the case – it is highly important that you mark your answers correctly in order to get credit.
An electronic scoring machine is often used in civil service offices because of the speed with which papers can be scored. Machine-scored answer sheets must be marked with a pencil, which will be given to you. This pencil has a high graphite content which responds to the electronic scoring machine. As a matter of fact, stray dots may register as answers, so do not let your pencil rest on the answer sheet while you are pondering the correct answer. Also, if your pencil lead breaks or is otherwise defective, ask for another.

Since the answer sheet will be dropped in a slot in the scoring machine, be careful not to bend the corners or get the paper crumpled.

The answer sheet normally has five vertical columns of numbers, with 30 numbers to a column. These numbers correspond to the question numbers in your test booklet. After each number, going across the page are four or five pairs of dotted lines. These short dotted lines have small letters or numbers above them. The first two pairs may also have a "T" or "F" above the letters. This indicates that the first two pairs only are to be used if the questions are of the true-false type. If the questions are multiple choice, disregard the "T" and "F" and pay attention only to the small letters or numbers.

Answer your questions in the manner of the sample that follows:

32. The largest city in the United States is
    A. Washington, D.C.
    B. New York City
    C. Chicago
    D. Detroit
    E. San Francisco

1) Choose the answer you think is best. (New York City is the largest, so "B" is correct.)
2) Find the row of dotted lines numbered the same as the question you are answering. (Find row number 32)
3) Find the pair of dotted lines corresponding to the answer. (Find the pair of lines under the mark "B.")
4) Make a solid black mark between the dotted lines.

VI. BEFORE THE TEST

Common sense will help you find procedures to follow to get ready for an examination. Too many of us, however, overlook these sensible measures. Indeed, nervousness and fatigue have been found to be the most serious reasons why applicants fail to do their best on civil service tests. Here is a list of reminders:

- Begin your preparation early – Don't wait until the last minute to go scurrying around for books and materials or to find out what the position is all about.
- Prepare continuously – An hour a night for a week is better than an all-night cram session. This has been definitely established. What is more, a night a week for a month will return better dividends than crowding your study into a shorter period of time.
- Locate the place of the exam – You have been sent a notice telling you when and where to report for the examination. If the location is in a different town or otherwise unfamiliar to you, it would be well to inquire the best route and learn something about the building.
- Relax the night before the test – Allow your mind to rest. Do not study at all that night. Plan some mild recreation or diversion; then go to bed early and get a good night's sleep.
- Get up early enough to make a leisurely trip to the place for the test – This way unforeseen events, traffic snarls, unfamiliar buildings, etc. will not upset you.
- Dress comfortably – A written test is not a fashion show. You will be known by number and not by name, so wear something comfortable.

- Leave excess paraphernalia at home – Shopping bags and odd bundles will get in your way. You need bring only the items mentioned in the official notice you received; usually everything you need is provided. Do not bring reference books to the exam. They will only confuse those last minutes and be taken away from you when in the test room.
- Arrive somewhat ahead of time – If because of transportation schedules you must get there very early, bring a newspaper or magazine to take your mind off yourself while waiting.
- Locate the examination room – When you have found the proper room, you will be directed to the seat or part of the room where you will sit. Sometimes you are given a sheet of instructions to read while you are waiting. Do not fill out any forms until you are told to do so; just read them and be prepared.
- Relax and prepare to listen to the instructions
- If you have any physical problem that may keep you from doing your best, be sure to tell the test administrator. If you are sick or in poor health, you really cannot do your best on the exam. You can come back and take the test some other time.

VII. AT THE TEST

The day of the test is here and you have the test booklet in your hand. The temptation to get going is very strong. Caution! There is more to success than knowing the right answers. You must know how to identify your papers and understand variations in the type of short-answer question used in this particular examination. Follow these suggestions for maximum results from your efforts:

1) Cooperate with the monitor

The test administrator has a duty to create a situation in which you can be as much at ease as possible. He will give instructions, tell you when to begin, check to see that you are marking your answer sheet correctly, and so on. He is not there to guard you, although he will see that your competitors do not take unfair advantage. He wants to help you do your best.

2) Listen to all instructions

Don't jump the gun! Wait until you understand all directions. In most civil service tests you get more time than you need to answer the questions. So don't be in a hurry. Read each word of instructions until you clearly understand the meaning. Study the examples, listen to all announcements and follow directions. Ask questions if you do not understand what to do.

3) Identify your papers

Civil service exams are usually identified by number only. You will be assigned a number; you must not put your name on your test papers. Be sure to copy your number correctly. Since more than one exam may be given, copy your exact examination title.

4) Plan your time

Unless you are told that a test is a "speed" or "rate of work" test, speed itself is usually not important. Time enough to answer all the questions will be provided, but this does not mean that you have all day. An overall time limit has been set. Divide the total time (in minutes) by the number of questions to determine the approximate time you have for each question.

5) Do not linger over difficult questions

If you come across a difficult question, mark it with a paper clip (useful to have along) and come back to it when you have been through the booklet. One caution if you do this – be sure to skip a number on your answer sheet as well. Check often to be sure that you have not lost your place and that you are marking in the row numbered the same as the question you are answering.

6) Read the questions

Be sure you know what the question asks! Many capable people are unsuccessful because they failed to *read* the questions correctly.

7) Answer all questions

Unless you have been instructed that a penalty will be deducted for incorrect answers, it is better to guess than to omit a question.

8) Speed tests

It is often better NOT to guess on speed tests. It has been found that on timed tests people are tempted to spend the last few seconds before time is called in marking answers at random – without even reading them – in the hope of picking up a few extra points. To discourage this practice, the instructions may warn you that your score will be "corrected" for guessing. That is, a penalty will be applied. The incorrect answers will be deducted from the correct ones, or some other penalty formula will be used.

9) Review your answers

If you finish before time is called, go back to the questions you guessed or omitted to give them further thought. Review other answers if you have time.

10) Return your test materials

If you are ready to leave before others have finished or time is called, take ALL your materials to the monitor and leave quietly. Never take any test material with you. The monitor can discover whose papers are not complete, and taking a test booklet may be grounds for disqualification.

VIII. EXAMINATION TECHNIQUES

1) Read the general instructions carefully. These are usually printed on the first page of the exam booklet. As a rule, these instructions refer to the timing of the examination; the fact that you should not start work until the signal and must stop work at a signal, etc. If there are any *special* instructions, such as a choice of questions to be answered, make sure that you note this instruction carefully.

2) When you are ready to start work on the examination, that is as soon as the signal has been given, read the instructions to each question booklet, underline any key words or phrases, such as *least, best, outline, describe* and the like. In this way you will tend to answer as requested rather than discover on reviewing your paper that you *listed without describing*, that you selected the *worst* choice rather than the *best* choice, etc.

3) If the examination is of the objective or multiple-choice type – that is, each question will also give a series of possible answers: A, B, C or D, and you are called upon to select the best answer and write the letter next to that answer on your answer paper – it is advisable to start answering each question in turn. There may be anywhere from 50 to 100 such questions in the three or four hours allotted and you can see how much time would be taken if you read through all the questions before beginning to answer any. Furthermore, if you come across a question or group of questions which you know would be difficult to answer, it would undoubtedly affect your handling of all the other questions.

4) If the examination is of the essay type and contains but a few questions, it is a moot point as to whether you should read all the questions before starting to answer any one. Of course, if you are given a choice – say five out of seven and the like – then it is essential to read all the questions so you can eliminate the two that are most difficult. If, however, you are asked to answer all the questions, there may be danger in trying to answer the easiest one first because you may find that you will spend too much time on it. The best technique is to answer the first question, then proceed to the second, etc.

5) Time your answers. Before the exam begins, write down the time it started, then add the time allowed for the examination and write down the time it must be completed, then divide the time available somewhat as follows:
    - If 3-1/2 hours are allowed, that would be 210 minutes. If you have 80 objective-type questions, that would be an average of 2-1/2 minutes per question. Allow yourself no more than 2 minutes per question, or a total of 160 minutes, which will permit about 50 minutes to review.
    - If for the time allotment of 210 minutes there are 7 essay questions to answer, that would average about 30 minutes a question. Give yourself only 25 minutes per question so that you have about 35 minutes to review.

6) The most important instruction is to *read each question* and make sure you know what is wanted. The second most important instruction is to *time yourself properly* so that you answer every question. The third most important instruction is to *answer every question*. Guess if you have to but include something for each question. Remember that you will receive no credit for a blank and will probably receive some credit if you write something in answer to an essay question. If you guess a letter – say "B" for a multiple-choice question – you may have guessed right. If you leave a blank as an answer to a multiple-choice question, the examiners may respect your feelings but it will not add a point to your score. Some exams may penalize you for wrong answers, so in such cases *only*, you may not want to guess unless you have some basis for your answer.

7) Suggestions
    a. Objective-type questions
        1. Examine the question booklet for proper sequence of pages and questions
        2. Read all instructions carefully
        3. Skip any question which seems too difficult; return to it after all other questions have been answered
        4. Apportion your time properly; do not spend too much time on any single question or group of questions

5. Note and underline key words – *all, most, fewest, least, best, worst, same, opposite*, etc.
6. Pay particular attention to negatives
7. Note unusual option, e.g., unduly long, short, complex, different or similar in content to the body of the question
8. Observe the use of "hedging" words – *probably, may, most likely*, etc.
9. Make sure that your answer is put next to the same number as the question
10. Do not second-guess unless you have good reason to believe the second answer is definitely more correct
11. Cross out original answer if you decide another answer is more accurate; do not erase until you are ready to hand your paper in
12. Answer all questions; guess unless instructed otherwise
13. Leave time for review

b. Essay questions
   1. Read each question carefully
   2. Determine exactly what is wanted. Underline key words or phrases.
   3. Decide on outline or paragraph answer
   4. Include many different points and elements unless asked to develop any one or two points or elements
   5. Show impartiality by giving pros and cons unless directed to select one side only
   6. Make and write down any assumptions you find necessary to answer the questions
   7. Watch your English, grammar, punctuation and choice of words
   8. Time your answers; don't crowd material

8) Answering the essay question

Most essay questions can be answered by framing the specific response around several key words or ideas. Here are a few such key words or ideas:

M's: manpower, materials, methods, money, management
P's: purpose, program, policy, plan, procedure, practice, problems, pitfalls, personnel, public relations
   a. Six basic steps in handling problems:
      1. Preliminary plan and background development
      2. Collect information, data and facts
      3. Analyze and interpret information, data and facts
      4. Analyze and develop solutions as well as make recommendations
      5. Prepare report and sell recommendations
      6. Install recommendations and follow up effectiveness

   b. Pitfalls to avoid
      1. *Taking things for granted* – A statement of the situation does not necessarily imply that each of the elements is necessarily true; for example, a complaint may be invalid and biased so that all that can be taken for granted is that a complaint has been registered

2. *Considering only one side of a situation* – Wherever possible, indicate several alternatives and then point out the reasons you selected the best one
3. *Failing to indicate follow up* – Whenever your answer indicates action on your part, make certain that you will take proper follow-up action to see how successful your recommendations, procedures or actions turn out to be
4. *Taking too long in answering any single question* – Remember to time your answers properly

IX. AFTER THE TEST

Scoring procedures differ in detail among civil service jurisdictions although the general principles are the same. Whether the papers are hand-scored or graded by machine we have described, they are nearly always graded by number. That is, the person who marks the paper knows only the number – never the name – of the applicant. Not until all the papers have been graded will they be matched with names. If other tests, such as training and experience or oral interview ratings have been given, scores will be combined. Different parts of the examination usually have different weights. For example, the written test might count 60 percent of the final grade, and a rating of training and experience 40 percent. In many jurisdictions, veterans will have a certain number of points added to their grades.

After the final grade has been determined, the names are placed in grade order and an eligible list is established. There are various methods for resolving ties between those who get the same final grade – probably the most common is to place first the name of the person whose application was received first. Job offers are made from the eligible list in the order the names appear on it. You will be notified of your grade and your rank as soon as all these computations have been made. This will be done as rapidly as possible.

People who are found to meet the requirements in the announcement are called "eligibles." Their names are put on a list of eligible candidates. An eligible's chances of getting a job depend on how high he stands on this list and how fast agencies are filling jobs from the list.

When a job is to be filled from a list of eligibles, the agency asks for the names of people on the list of eligibles for that job. When the civil service commission receives this request, it sends to the agency the names of the three people highest on this list. Or, if the job to be filled has specialized requirements, the office sends the agency the names of the top three persons who meet these requirements from the general list.

The appointing officer makes a choice from among the three people whose names were sent to him. If the selected person accepts the appointment, the names of the others are put back on the list to be considered for future openings.

That is the rule in hiring from all kinds of eligible lists, whether they are for typist, carpenter, chemist, or something else. For every vacancy, the appointing officer has his choice of any one of the top three eligibles on the list. This explains why the person whose name is on top of the list sometimes does not get an appointment when some of the persons lower on the list do. If the appointing officer chooses the second or third eligible, the No. 1 eligible does not get a job at once, but stays on the list until he is appointed or the list is terminated.

X. HOW TO PASS THE INTERVIEW TEST

The examination for which you applied requires an oral interview test. You have already taken the written test and you are now being called for the interview test – the final part of the formal examination.

You may think that it is not possible to prepare for an interview test and that there are no procedures to follow during an interview. Our purpose is to point out some things you can do in advance that will help you and some good rules to follow and pitfalls to avoid while you are being interviewed.

What is an interview supposed to test?

The written examination is designed to test the technical knowledge and competence of the candidate; the oral is designed to evaluate intangible qualities, not readily measured otherwise, and to establish a list showing the relative fitness of each candidate – as measured against his competitors – for the position sought. Scoring is not on the basis of "right" and "wrong," but on a sliding scale of values ranging from "not passable" to "outstanding." As a matter of fact, it is possible to achieve a relatively low score without a single "incorrect" answer because of evident weakness in the qualities being measured.

Occasionally, an examination may consist entirely of an oral test – either an individual or a group oral. In such cases, information is sought concerning the technical knowledges and abilities of the candidate, since there has been no written examination for this purpose. More commonly, however, an oral test is used to supplement a written examination.

Who conducts interviews?

The composition of oral boards varies among different jurisdictions. In nearly all, a representative of the personnel department serves as chairman. One of the members of the board may be a representative of the department in which the candidate would work. In some cases, "outside experts" are used, and, frequently, a businessman or some other representative of the general public is asked to serve. Labor and management or other special groups may be represented. The aim is to secure the services of experts in the appropriate field.

However the board is composed, it is a good idea (and not at all improper or unethical) to ascertain in advance of the interview who the members are and what groups they represent. When you are introduced to them, you will have some idea of their backgrounds and interests, and at least you will not stutter and stammer over their names.

What should be done before the interview?

While knowledge about the board members is useful and takes some of the surprise element out of the interview, there is other preparation which is more substantive. It *is* possible to prepare for an oral interview – in several ways:

1) Keep a copy of your application and review it carefully before the interview

This may be the only document before the oral board, and the starting point of the interview. Know what education and experience you have listed there, and the sequence and dates of all of it. Sometimes the board will ask you to review the highlights of your experience for them; you should not have to hem and haw doing it.

2) Study the class specification and the examination announcement

Usually, the oral board has one or both of these to guide them. The qualities, characteristics or knowledges required by the position sought are stated in these documents. They offer valuable clues as to the nature of the oral interview. For example, if the job involves supervisory responsibilities, the announcement will usually indicate that knowledge of modern supervisory methods and the qualifications of the candidate as a supervisor will be tested. If so, you can expect such questions, frequently in the form of a hypothetical situation which you are expected to solve. NEVER go into an oral without knowledge of the duties and responsibilities of the job you seek.

3) Think through each qualification required

Try to visualize the kind of questions you would ask if you were a board member. How well could you answer them? Try especially to appraise your own knowledge and background in each area, *measured against the job sought*, and identify any areas in which you are weak. Be critical and realistic – do not flatter yourself.

4) Do some general reading in areas in which you feel you may be weak

For example, if the job involves supervision and your past experience has NOT, some general reading in supervisory methods and practices, particularly in the field of human relations, might be useful. Do NOT study agency procedures or detailed manuals. The oral board will be testing your understanding and capacity, not your memory.

5) Get a good night's sleep and watch your general health and mental attitude

You will want a clear head at the interview. Take care of a cold or any other minor ailment, and of course, no hangovers.

What should be done on the day of the interview?

Now comes the day of the interview itself. Give yourself plenty of time to get there. Plan to arrive somewhat ahead of the scheduled time, particularly if your appointment is in the fore part of the day. If a previous candidate fails to appear, the board might be ready for you a bit early. By early afternoon an oral board is almost invariably behind schedule if there are many candidates, and you may have to wait. Take along a book or magazine to read, or your application to review, but leave any extraneous material in the waiting room when you go in for your interview. In any event, relax and compose yourself.

The matter of dress is important. The board is forming impressions about you – from your experience, your manners, your attitude, and your appearance. Give your personal appearance careful attention. Dress your best, but not your flashiest. Choose conservative, appropriate clothing, and be sure it is immaculate. This is a business interview, and your appearance should indicate that you regard it as such. Besides, being well groomed and properly dressed will help boost your confidence.

Sooner or later, someone will call your name and escort you into the interview room. *This is it.* From here on you are on your own. It is too late for any more preparation. But remember, you asked for this opportunity to prove your fitness, and you are here because your request was granted.

What happens when you go in?

The usual sequence of events will be as follows: The clerk (who is often the board stenographer) will introduce you to the chairman of the oral board, who will introduce you to the other members of the board. Acknowledge the introductions before you sit down. Do not be surprised if you find a microphone facing you or a stenotypist sitting by. Oral interviews are usually recorded in the event of an appeal or other review.

Usually the chairman of the board will open the interview by reviewing the highlights of your education and work experience from your application – primarily for the benefit of the other members of the board, as well as to get the material into the record. Do not interrupt or comment unless there is an error or significant misinterpretation; if that is the case, do not hesitate. But do not quibble about insignificant matters. Also, he will usually ask you some question about your education, experience or your present job – partly to get you to start talking and to establish the interviewing "rapport." He may start the actual questioning, or turn it over to one of the other members. Frequently, each member undertakes the questioning on a particular area, one in which he is perhaps most competent, so you can expect each member to participate in the examination. Because time is limited, you may also expect some rather abrupt switches in the direction the questioning takes, so do not be upset by it. Normally, a board member will not pursue a single line of questioning unless he discovers a particular strength or weakness.

After each member has participated, the chairman will usually ask whether any member has any further questions, then will ask you if you have anything you wish to add. Unless you are expecting this question, it may floor you. Worse, it may start you off on an extended, extemporaneous speech. The board is not usually seeking more information. The question is principally to offer you a last opportunity to present further qualifications or to indicate that you have nothing to add. So, if you feel that a significant qualification or characteristic has been overlooked, it is proper to point it out in a sentence or so. Do not compliment the board on the thoroughness of their examination – they have been sketchy, and you know it. If you wish, merely say, "No thank you, I have nothing further to add." This is a point where you can "talk yourself out" of a good impression or fail to present an important bit of information. Remember, *you close the interview yourself.*

The chairman will then say, "That is all, Mr. _____, thank you." Do not be startled; the interview is over, and quicker than you think. Thank him, gather your belongings and take your leave. Save your sigh of relief for the other side of the door.

How to put your best foot forward

Throughout this entire process, you may feel that the board individually and collectively is trying to pierce your defenses, seek out your hidden weaknesses and embarrass and confuse you. Actually, this is not true. They are obliged to make an appraisal of your qualifications for the job you are seeking, and they want to see you in your best light. Remember, they must interview all candidates and a non-cooperative candidate may become a failure in spite of their best efforts to bring out his qualifications. Here are 15 suggestions that will help you:

1) Be natural – Keep your attitude confident, not cocky

If you are not confident that you can do the job, do not expect the board to be. Do not apologize for your weaknesses, try to bring out your strong points. The board is interested in a positive, not negative, presentation. Cockiness will antagonize any board member and make him wonder if you are covering up a weakness by a false show of strength.

2) Get comfortable, but don't lounge or sprawl

Sit erectly but not stiffly. A careless posture may lead the board to conclude that you are careless in other things, or at least that you are not impressed by the importance of the occasion. Either conclusion is natural, even if incorrect. Do not fuss with your clothing, a pencil or an ashtray. Your hands may occasionally be useful to emphasize a point; do not let them become a point of distraction.

3) Do not wisecrack or make small talk

This is a serious situation, and your attitude should show that you consider it as such. Further, the time of the board is limited – they do not want to waste it, and neither should you.

4) Do not exaggerate your experience or abilities
In the first place, from information in the application or other interviews and sources, the board may know more about you than you think. Secondly, you probably will not get away with it. An experienced board is rather adept at spotting such a situation, so do not take the chance.

5) If you know a board member, do not make a point of it, yet do not hide it
Certainly you are not fooling him, and probably not the other members of the board. Do not try to take advantage of your acquaintanceship – it will probably do you little good.

6) Do not dominate the interview
Let the board do that. They will give you the clues – do not assume that you have to do all the talking. Realize that the board has a number of questions to ask you, and do not try to take up all the interview time by showing off your extensive knowledge of the answer to the first one.

7) Be attentive
You only have 20 minutes or so, and you should keep your attention at its sharpest throughout. When a member is addressing a problem or question to you, give him your undivided attention. Address your reply principally to him, but do not exclude the other board members.

8) Do not interrupt
A board member may be stating a problem for you to analyze. He will ask you a question when the time comes. Let him state the problem, and wait for the question.

9) Make sure you understand the question
Do not try to answer until you are sure what the question is. If it is not clear, restate it in your own words or ask the board member to clarify it for you. However, do not haggle about minor elements.

10) Reply promptly but not hastily
A common entry on oral board rating sheets is "candidate responded readily," or "candidate hesitated in replies." Respond as promptly and quickly as you can, but do not jump to a hasty, ill-considered answer.

11) Do not be peremptory in your answers
A brief answer is proper – but do not fire your answer back. That is a losing game from your point of view. The board member can probably ask questions much faster than you can answer them.

12) Do not try to create the answer you think the board member wants
He is interested in what kind of mind you have and how it works – not in playing games. Furthermore, he can usually spot this practice and will actually grade you down on it.

13) Do not switch sides in your reply merely to agree with a board member
Frequently, a member will take a contrary position merely to draw you out and to see if you are willing and able to defend your point of view. Do not start a debate, yet do not surrender a good position. If a position is worth taking, it is worth defending.

14) Do not be afraid to admit an error in judgment if you are shown to be wrong

The board knows that you are forced to reply without any opportunity for careful consideration. Your answer may be demonstrably wrong. If so, admit it and get on with the interview.

15) Do not dwell at length on your present job

The opening question may relate to your present assignment. Answer the question but do not go into an extended discussion. You are being examined for a *new* job, not your present one. As a matter of fact, try to phrase ALL your answers in terms of the job for which you are being examined.

Basis of Rating

Probably you will forget most of these "do's" and "don'ts" when you walk into the oral interview room. Even remembering them all will not ensure you a passing grade. Perhaps you did not have the qualifications in the first place. But remembering them will help you to put your best foot forward, without treading on the toes of the board members.

Rumor and popular opinion to the contrary notwithstanding, an oral board wants you to make the best appearance possible. They know you are under pressure – but they also want to see how you respond to it as a guide to what your reaction would be under the pressures of the job you seek. They will be influenced by the degree of poise you display, the personal traits you show and the manner in which you respond.

ABOUT THIS BOOK

This book contains tests divided into Examination Sections. Go through each test, answering every question in the margin. We have also attached a sample answer sheet at the back of the book that can be removed and used. At the end of each test look at the answer key and check your answers. On the ones you got wrong, look at the right answer choice and learn. Do not fill in the answers first. Do not memorize the questions and answers, but understand the answer and principles involved. On your test, the questions will likely be different from the samples. Questions are changed and new ones added. If you understand these past questions you should have success with any changes that arise. Tests may consist of several types of questions. We have additional books on each subject should more study be advisable or necessary for you. Finally, the more you study, the better prepared you will be. This book is intended to be the last thing you study before you walk into the examination room. Prior study of relevant texts is also recommended. NLC publishes some of these in our Fundamental Series. Knowledge and good sense are important factors in passing your exam. Good luck also helps. So now study this Passbook, absorb the material contained within and take that knowledge into the examination. Then do your best to pass that exam.

EXAMINATION SECTION

EXAMINATION SECTION
TEST 1

DIRECTIONS: Each question or incomplete statement is followed by several suggested answers or completions. Select the one that BEST answers the question or completes the Statement. *PRINT THE LETTER OF THE CORRECT ANSWER IN THE SPACE AT THE RIGHT.*

Questions 1-5.

DIRECTIONS: Answer questions 1 through 5 on the basis of the following passage.

Mental disorders are found in a fairly large number of the inmates in correctional institutions. There are no exact figures as to the inmates who are mentally disturbed -- partly because it is hard to draw a precise line between "mental disturbance" and "normality" -- but 'experts find that somewhere between 15% and 25% of inmates are suffering from disorders that are obvious enough to show up in routine psychiatric examinations. Society has not yet really come to grips with the problem of what to do with mentally disturbed offenders. There is not enough money available to set up treatment programs for all the people identified as mentally disturbed; and there would probably not be enough qualified psychiatric personnel available to run such programs even if they could be set up. Most mentally disturbed offenders are therefore left to serve out their time in correctional institutions, and the burden of dealing with them falls on correction officers. This means that a correction offcer must be sensitive enough to human behavior to know when he is dealing with a person who is not mentally normal, and that the officer must be imaginative enough to be able to sense how an abnormal individual might react under certain circumstances.

1. According to the above passage, mentally disturbed inmakes in correctional institutions　　1.____

    A. are usually transferred to mental hospitals when their condition is noticed
    B. cannot be told from other inmates, because tests cannot distinguish between insane people and normal people
    C. may constitute as mich as 25% of the total inmate population
    D. should be regarded as no different from all the other inmates

2. The passage says that today the job of handling mentally disturbed inmates is MAINLY up to　　2.____

    A. psychiatric personnel　　　　B. other inmates
    C. correction officers　　　　　D. administrative officials

3. Of the following, which is a reason given in the passage for society's failure to provide adequate treatment programs for mentally disturbed inmates?　　3.____

    A. Law-abiding citizens should not have to pay for fancy treatment programs for criminals.
    B. A person who breaks the law should not expect society to give him special help.
    C. It is impossible to tell whether an inmate is mentally disturbed.
    D. There are not enough trained people to provide the kind of treatment needed.

4. The expression *abnormal individual,* as used in the last sentence of the passage, refers to an individual who is

   A. of average intelligence
   B. of superior intelligence
   C. completely normal
   D. mentally disturbed

5. The reader of the passage would MOST likely agree that

   A. correction officers should not expect mentally disturbed persons to behave the same way a normal person would behave
   B. correction officers should not report infractions of the rules committed by mentally disturbed persons
   C. mentally disturbed persons who break the law should be treated exactly the same way as anyone else
   D. mentally disturbed persons who have broken the law should not be imprisoned

Questions 6-12.

DIRECTIONS: Questions 6 through 12 are based on the roster of patients, the instructions, the table, and the sample question given below.

Twelve patients of a mental institution are divided into three permanent groups in their workshop. They must be present and accounted for in these groups at the beginning of each workday. During the day, the patients check out of their groups for various activities. They check back in again when those activities have been completed. Assume that the day is divided into three activity periods.

ROSTER OF PATIENTS

GROUP X	Ted	Frank	George	Harry
GROUP Y	Jack	Ken	Larry	Mel
GROUP Z	Phil	Bob	Sam	Vic

The following table shows the movements of these patients from their groups during the day. Assume that all were present and accounted for at the beginning of Period I.

		GROUP X	GROUP Y	GROUP Z
Period I	Check-outs	Ted, Frank	Ken, Larry	Phil
Period II	Check-ins	Frank	Ken, Larry	Phil
	Check-outs	George	Jack, Mel	Bob, Sam, Vic
Period III	Check-ins	George	Mel, Jack	Sam, Bob, Vic
	Check-outs	Frank, Harry	Ken	Vic

SAMPLE QUESTION: At the end of Period II, the patients remaining in Group X were

   A. Ted, Frank, Harry
   B. Frank, Harry
   C. Ted, George
   D. Frank, Harry, George

During Period I, Ted and Frank were checked out from Group X. During Period II, Frank was checked back in and George was checked out. Therefore, the members of the group remaining out are Ted and George. The two other members of the group, Frank and Harry, should be present. The CORRECT answer is B.

6. At the end of Period I, the TOTAL number of patients remaining in their own permanent groups was

   A. 8   B. 7   C. 6   D. 5

7. At the end of Period I, the patients remaining in Group Z were

   A. George and Harry
   B. Jack and Mel
   C. Bob, Sam, and Vic
   D. Phil

8. At the end of Period II, the patients remaining in Group Y were

   A. Ken and Larry
   B. Jack, Ken, and Mel
   C. Jack and Ken
   D. Ken, Mel, and Larry

9. At the end of Period II, the TOTAL number of patients remaining in their own permanent groups was

   A. 8   B. 7   C. 6   D. 5

10. At the end of Period II, the patients who were NOT present in Group Z were

    A. Phil, Bob, and Sam
    B. Sam, Bob, and Vic
    C. Sam, Vic, and Phil
    D. Vic, Phil, and Bob

11. At the end of Period II, the patients remaining in Group Y were

    A. Ted, Frank, and George
    B. Jack, Mel, and Ken
    C. Jack, Larry, and Mel
    D. Frank and Harry

12. At the end of Period III, the TOTAL number of patients NOT present in their own permanent groups was

    A. 4   B. 5   C. 6   D. 7

13. The one of the following conditions which bears no causative relationship to feeblemindedness is

    A. heredity
    B. cerebral defect
    C. early postnatal trauma
    D. dementia

14. Physical conditions which are caused by emotional conflicts are generally referred to as being

    A. psycho-social
    B. hypochondriacal
    C. psychosomatic
    D. psychotic

15. Of the following conditions, the one in which anxiety is NOT generally found is

    A. psychopathic personality
    B. mild hysteria
    C. psychoneurosis
    D. compulsive-obsessive personality

16. Kleptomania may BEST be described as a

    A. neurotic drive to accumulate personal property through compulsive acts in order to dispose of it to others with whom one wishes friendship
    B. type of neurosis which manifests itself in an uncontrollable impulse to steal without economic motivation
    C. psychopathic trait which is probably hereditary in nature
    D. manifestation of punishment-inviting behavior based upon guilt feelings for some other crime or wrong-doing, fantasied or real, committed as a child

17. The one of the following tests which is NOT ordinarily used as a protective technique is the

    A. Wechsler Bellevue Scale
    B. Rorschach Test
    C. Thematic Apperception Test
    D. Jung Free Association Test

18. The outstanding personality test in use at the present time is the Rorschach Test. Of the following considerations, the GREATEST value of this test to the psychiatrist and social worker is that it

    A. provides practical recommendations with reference to further educational and vocational training possibilities for the person tested
    B. reveals in quick, concise form the hereditary factors affecting the individual personality
    C. helps in substantiating a diagnosis of juvenile delinquency
    D. helps in a diagnostic formulation and in determining differential treatment

19. Of the following, the one through which ethical values are MOST generally acquired is

    A. heredity
    B. early training in school
    C. admonition and strict corrective measures by parents and other supervising adults
    D. integration into the self of parental values and attitudes

20. Delinquent behavior is MOST generally a result of

    A. living and growing up in an environment that is both socially and financially deprived
    B. a lack of educational opportunity for development of individual skills
    C. multiple factors -- psychological, bio-social, emotional and environmental
    D. low frustration tolerance of many parents toward problems of married life

21. Alcoholism in the United States is USUALLY caused by

    A. the sense of frustration in one's work
    B. inadequacy of recreational facilities
    C. neurotic conflicts expressed in drinking excessively
    D. shyness and timidity

22. The MOST distinctive characteristic of the chronic alcoholic is that he drinks alcohol   22.____

    A. socially   B. compulsively
    C. periodically   D. secretly

23. The chronic alcoholic is the person who cannot face reality without alcohol, and yet   23.____
    whose adequate adjustment to reality is impossible so long as he uses alcohol.
    On the basis of this statement, it is MOST reasonable to conclude that individuals
    overindulge in alcohol because alcohol

    A. deadens the sense of conflict, giving the individual an illusion of social competence
       and a feeling of well-being and success
    B. provides the individual with an outlet to display his feelings of good-fellowship and
       cheerfulness which are characteristic of his extroverted personality
    C. affords an escape technique from habitual irrational fears, but does not affect rational fears
    D. offers an escape from imagery and feelings of superiority which cause tension and
       anxiety

24. The one of the following drugs to which a person is LEAST likely to become addicted is   24.____

    A. opium   B. morphine   C. marijuana   D. heroin

25. Teenagers who become addicted to the use of drugs are MOST generally   25.____

    A. mentally defective   B. paranoid
    C. normally adventurous   D. emotionally disturbed

26. In the light of the current high rate of addiction to drugs among youths throughout the   26.____
    country, the one of the following statements which is generally considered to be LEAST
    correct is that

    A. a relatively large number of children and youths who experiment with drugs
       become addicts
    B. youths who use narcotics do so because of some emotional and personality disturbance
    C. youthful addicts are found largely among those who suffer to an abnormal extent
       deprivations in their personal development and growth
    D. the great majority of youthful addicts have had unfortunate home experiences and
       practically no contact with established community agencies

27. The one of the following terms which BEST describes the psychological desire to repeat   27.____
    the use of a drug intermittently or continously because of emotional needs is

    A. habituation   B. euphoria   C. tolerance   D. addiction

28. The desire for special clothing in a mental institution usually is concerned with   28.____

    A. shoes   B. sox   C. trousers   D. underwear

29. A study entitled *"A preliminary evaluation of the relationship between group psychother-*   29.____
    apy and the adjustment of adolescent inmates (16-21 years) in a short-term penal institu-
    tion" was conducted by the Diagnostic Staff at Rikers Island in New York. A conclusion
    which was drawn as a result of the study was that

A. a repetition of the study was necessary with smaller therapy and non-therapy groups
B. group psychotherapy subjects displayed a better institutional adjustment than those not receiving group therapy
C. no follow-up study was necessary because of the negative results from the original study
D. a smaller proportion of experimental group subjects improved after receiving group psychotherapy when compared to those who did not receive group therapy

30. The one of the following statements which is MOST accurate concerning group psychotherapy is that group psychotherapy

    A. is in a way an outgrowth of the concept of patient self-government
    B. is of little value with deviant personality types
    C. should make the group members resent help from their fellow patients
    D. reflects a punitive rather than a rehabilitative aim

31. In group counseling and psychotherapy it is USUALLY true that persons are more defensive and argumentative than in individualized counseling and therapy sessions. The reason for this tendency is that

    A. individuals in a group setting feel it more necessary to protect their personality
    B. people in group settings are motivated by the characteristically free atmosphere
    C. people would rather argue in a group setting than in an individualized setting
    D. the group session is more poorly organized and therefore uncontrolled

32. There is a group of mentally ill patients who have a <u>functional psychosis.</u>
The word "functional" in this case indicates that

    A. it is an organic psychosis
    B. the psychosis is caused by alcoholism or drug addiction
    C. there are no demonstrable changes in the brain
    D. there are clinical findings of senile arteriosclerosis

33. "Sociopaths" is a fairly new word used to describe

    A. confirmed narcotics addicts
    B. latent male homosexuals
    C. neurotic adolescents
    D. psychopathic personalities

34. The incarceration of the geriatric presents many problems in mental administration. The word "geriatric" means MOST NEARLY

    A. dipsomanic (alcoholic)
    B. moronic (mentally deficient)
    C. pertaining to split personality types
    D. pertaining to individuals of advanced years

35. Jobs for ex-patients can MOST often be found in

    A. big corporations
    B. domestic service
    C. government agencies
    D. small private enterprises

KEY (CORRECT ANSWERS)

1. C
2. C
3. D
4. D
5. A

6. B
7. C
8. A
9. D
10. B

11. C
12. B
13. D
14. C
15. A

16. B
17. A
18. D
19. D
20. C

21. C
22. B
23. A
24. C
25. D

26. A
27. A
28. A
29. B
30. A

31. A
32. C
33. D
34. D
35. D

———

EXAMINATION SECTION
TEST 1

DIRECTIONS: Each question or incomplete statement is followed by several suggested answers or completions. Select the one that BEST answers the question or completes the statement. *PRINT THE LETTER OF THE CORRECT ANSWER IN THE SPACE AT THE RIGHT.*

1. A relationship in which a patient becomes dependent on the nurse 1.____
    - A. is always unprofessional
    - B. is inevitably "bad" for the patient
    - C. may be necessary temporarily
    - D. impedes learning

2. Anxiety is the CHIEF characteristic of the 2.____
    - A. immature personality
    - B. psychoneurotic disorder
    - C. involutional psychotic reaction
    - D. mentally retarded adolescent

3. The mode of psychological adjustment known as regression can BEST be described as 3.____
    - A. refusing to think of unpleasant situations
    - B. changing to a type of behavior which is characteristic of an earlier period in life
    - C. reverting to actions characteristic of an historically early or primitive code of behavior
    - D. hostility towards persons or objects that prove frustrating

4. The CHIEF danger in the employment of escape mechanisms as a form of adjustment is that they 4.____
    - A. do more harm than good
    - B. are socially undesirable
    - C. make the experience expensive
    - D. leave the basic problem unsolved

5. In essential hypertension, there is a(n) 5.____
    - A. *increase* in systolic pressure and a *decrease* in diastolic pressure
    - B. *decrease* in systolic pressure and an *increase* in diastolic pressure
    - C. *increase* in *both* systolic and diastolic pressure
    - D. *decrease* in *both* systolic and diastolic pressure

6. The *initial* paralysis in cerebral vascular accident, regardless of cause, is the type known as 6.____
    - A. spastic B. paraplegic C. flaccid D. rigid

7. Cerebral hemorrhage *most frequently* occurs in males in the age range from 7.____
    - A. 20 to 30 years
    - B. 30 to 40 years
    - C. 40 to 50 years
    - D. 50 years and over

8. Hereditary progressive muscular dystrophy is a disease characterized by progressive weakness and final atrophy of groups of muscles.
Of the following statements about muscular dystrophy, the one which is LEAST accurate is that

   A. there is no known cure for muscular dystrophy at present
   B. muscular dystrophy is a disease of the central nervous system
   C. early signs of muscular dystrophy are frequent falls, difficulty climbing stairs, development of lordosis, and a waddling gait
   D. therapeutic exercises may have some temporary value in the treatment of muscular dystrophy

9. The home care program is an extension of the hospital's service into the home on an extra-mural basis.
Of the following statements, the one that BEST explains the success of this program is that it

   A. *recognizes* the value to the patient and his family of the preservation of normal family life despite the limitations imposed by the patient's illness
   B. *makes* more hospital beds available for acute illnesses and emergency care
   C. reduces the cost of hospital care by reducing the number of inpatients
   D. *simplifies* hospital administration by reducing the number of chronically ill in hospitals

10. The MOST important of the following reasons for the rehabilitation of the seriously handicapped individual is that

    A. hospitalization of the handicapped is usually prolonged and costly to the community
    B. beds occupied by such patients reduce the number of hospital beds available for acutely ill patients
    C. care of chronically ill or handicapped patients is taxing and difficult for the family, the nurse, and the doctor
    D. it is important to the patient that he be as independent and useful as possible

11. There has been a notable increase in the discharge rate from mental institutions in the state during recent years. This change in statistics may be attributed CHIEFLY to

    A. increasing use of psychoanalysis and better trained personnel
    B. new drugs, changes in admission procedures, and the "open door" policy
    C. the increase in nursing homes for the elderly
    D. the use of psychotherapeutics and early diagnosis of mental illness

12. The PRINCIPAL and BASIC objective of mental hygiene is to

    A. modify attitudes as well as unhealthy behavior secondary to unhealthy attitudes
    B. care for the post-hospitalized psychiatric patient at home
    C. increase mental hygiene clinic services
    D. stimulate interest in improved education for doctors, nurses, and teachers

13. Separation of a child from his own home and placement in a foster home often arouses adverse reactions in the child. Of the following, the one which is MOST serious for the child is

    A. homesickness
    B. withdrawn behavior
    C. rebellion against authority
    D. dislike of new people

14. Behavior problems of the adolescent school child can BEST be explained by the fact that

    A. the adolescent suddenly becomes aware of the opposite sex at this time
    B. the demands made on adolescents by intolerant parents create rebellion against authority
    C. during childhood there is a general disregard of the child's need for independence by parents and other adults
    D. adolescence is a transition period between childhood and adulthood which usually creates feelings of insecurity in the adolescent

15. Of the following, the behavior which is LEAST indicative of serious emotional maladjustment in an adolescent boy is

    A. lying and cheating
    B. shyness and daydreaming
    C. gross overweight
    D. association with a teen-age gang

16. The one of the following diseases which is caused by a birth injury is

    A. cerebral palsy
    B. meningitis
    C. hydrocele
    D. congenital syphilis
    E. epilepsy

17. A delusion is a

    A. disharmony of mind and body
    B. fantastic image formed during sleep
    C. false judgment of objective things
    D. cessation of thought
    E. distorted perception or image

18. The one of the following which is the MOST common form of treatment employed by psychiatrists in treating patients with mental disorders is

    A. hypnotism
    B. hydrotherapy
    C. electroshock
    D. insulin shock
    E. psychotherapy

19. A masochistic person is one who

    A. is very melancholy
    B. has delusions of grandeur about himself
    C. derives pleasure from being cruelly treated
    D. believes in a fatalistic philosophy
    E. derives pleasure from hurting another

20. Surgery is *ESPECIALLY* difficult during the Oedipal period because of the

    A. father attachment
    B. mental age
    C. castration anxieties
    D. rejection complex
    E. separation from siblings

21. A psychometric test is one which attempts to measure

    A. social adjustment
    B. emotional maturity
    C. physical activity
    D. personality development
    E. Intellectual capacity

22. The one of the following conditions which falls into the classification of a psychosis rather than psychoneurosis is

    A. anxiety hysteria
    B. schizophrenia
    C. neurasthenia
    D. convesion hysteria
    E. compulsion neurosis

23. The one of the following which BEST describes psychosomatic medicine is:

    A. The understanding and treatment of both mind and body in illness
    B. The treatment of disease by psychiatric methods only
    C. The separation of mind and body in medical treatment
    D. The psychological testing of all individuals
    E. A system of socialized medical planning

24. The one of the following conditions for which shock treatment is *FREQUENTLY* used is

    A. alcoholism
    B. Parkinson's syndrome
    C. multiple sclerosis
    D. schizophrenia
    E. diabetes

25. The one of the following conditions which is *NOT* caused by the dysfunction of endocrine glands is

    A. myxedema
    B. duodenal ulcer
    C. cretinism
    D. Addison's disease
    E. none of the above

KEY (CORRECT ANSWERS)

1. C
2. B
3. B
4. D
5. C

6. C
7. D
8. B
9. A
10. D

11. B
12. A
13. B
14. D
15. D

16. A
17. C
18. E
19. C
20. C

21. E
22. B
23. A
24. D
25. B

———

TEST 2

DIRECTIONS: Each question or incomplete statement is followed by several suggested answers or completions. Select the one that BEST answers the question or completes the statement. *PRINT THE LETTER OF THE CORRECT ANSWER IN THE SPACE AT THE RIGHT.*

1. Euphoria is a state of

    A. depression   B. elation   C. ideation   D. frustration

2. An ailment found only in older people is

    A. manic depression   B. dementia praecox
    C. senile dementia   D. tabes dorsalis

3. The permissive policy employed in some mental hospitals is associated with a(n)

    A. increase in assaultive behavior
    B. open door policy
    C. decrease in the use of physical restraint
    D. increase in the use of physical restraint

4. A symptom of dementia praecox is

    A. extroversion   B. tic paralysis
    C. unpredictability   D. cerebral hemorrhage

5. Substituting an activity in which a person can succeed for one in which he may fail is

    A. sublimation   B. projection
    C. rationalization   D. compensation

6. Rationalization is the result of

    A. believing what one wants to believe
    B. reflective thinking
    C. scientific thinking
    D. basing conclusions on fact

7. Delusions of persecution are typical of

    A. epilepsy   B. regression
    C. schizophrenia   D. paranoia

8. A person with an IQ of 85 would be classified as

    A. defective   B. normal
    C. dull average   D. borderline

9. The term describing physical symptoms that do not arise *ENTIRELY* from physical causes is

    A. organic   B. psychoneurotic
    C. psychosomatic   D. psychopathological

10. The mechanism of attributing one's own ideas to others is termed

    A. projection
    B. substitution
    C. sublimation
    D. rationalization

11. A child's tendency to pattern after his parents is known as

    A. identification
    B. projection
    C. compensation
    D. substitution

12. Stuttering in children USUALLY originates from

    A. physical handicap
    B. mentally deficient parents
    C. emotional handicap
    D. imitation of other stutterers

13. Acute intoxication may PROPERLY be labeled a psychosis because it involves

    A. intellectual limitations
    B. emotional inadequacies
    C. bodily disease
    D. a severe loss of contact with reality

14. The outstanding change, of the following, in the aging process is that the aged are

    A. irritable
    B. no longer self-reliant
    C. senile
    D. easily influenced by stress

15. Re-adjusting the older person to be somewhat self-sufficient is known as

    A. stabilization
    B. regeneration
    C. rejuvenation
    D. rehabilitation

16. The spastic child usually

    A. is mentally retarded
    B. is potentially schizophrenic
    C. requires speech training
    D. has poor vision

17. Insomnia refers to

    A. unconsciousness
    B. sleeplessness
    C. sleep walking
    D. insensibility

18. A drug recently introduced in the treatment of mental illness is

    A. streptomycin
    B. paramino-salicylic acid
    C. reserpine
    D. cortisone

19. In general, the sleep requirement for an aged person as compared to the sleep requirement for a young adult is

    A. less
    B. more
    C. the same
    D. slightly greater

20. The MOST IMPORTANT aspect of the rehabilitation of a person who has suffered a stroke is the

    A. patient's emotional reaction to self
    B. doctor's attitude toward the patient
    C. nurse's attitude toward the patient
    D. family reaction toward the patient

21. If a patient tells a nurse that he is contemplating committing suicide, the nurse should   21.____

    A. not pay any attention, since people who threaten suicide seldom follow through
    B. urge him to consult a psychiatrist, since potential suicides need psychiatric help immediately
    C. be sympathetic. Her sympathy will divert him from his intention
    D. realize that he is a neurotic with whom she will try to work

22. The BEST advice you can give parents disturbed by their five-year-old child's habit of nailbiting is to tell them to   22.____

    A. find out what some of the pressures on the child are and try to relieve them
    B. paint the child's fingers with the product "bitter aloes"
    C. point out to the child that this is a baby habit and not desirable in a school child
    D. punish the child by not allowing him to watch television or go to the movies

23. In certain periods of development, anti-social behavior in young children is considered normal. However, of the following situations, the one which merits referral to a mental hygiene clinic is where   23.____

    A. a two-year-old persists in hitting his four- year-old brother
    B. a three-year-old develops enuresis when a new baby is brought into the home
    C. a four-year-old runs away from home at every opportunity
    D. a six-year-old is not friendly, has no "pals" after six months in school, and participates in activities only when compelled to

24. Learning occurs   24.____

    A. when the child's responses are adequate
    B. when a solution to the situation is obvious
    C. when the adult solves the problems
    D. None of the above

25. The FIRST emotions to become differentiated may be described as   25.____

    A. anger and fear   B. anger and distress
    C. fear and delight   D. delight and distress

KEY (CORRECT ANSWERS)

1. B
2. C
3. B
4. C
5. D

6. A
7. D
8. C
9. C
10. A

11. A
12. C
13. D
14. D
15. D

16. C
17. B
18. C
19. A
20. A

21. B
22. A
23. D
24. A
25. D

EXAMINATION SECTION
TEST 1

DIRECTIONS: Each question or incomplete statement is followed by several suggested answers or completions. Select the one that BEST answers the question or completes the statement. *PRINT THE LETTER OF THE CORRECT ANSWER IN THE SPACE AT THE RIGHT.*

1. The one of the following diseases which is the LEADING cause of death in the 10-to-15 year age group is
   A. cancer   B. tuberculosis   C. poliomyelitis
   D. diabetes   E. rheumatic fever

   1.____

2. The one of the following which would MOST likely be a result of untreated syphilis is
   A. paresis   B. phlebitis   C. carcinoma
   D. silicosis   E. angina pectoris

   2.____

3. The one of the following which is MOST likely to be used in establishing a diagnosis of epilepsy is a(n)
   A. electrocardiogram   B. spinal x-ray
   C. fluoroscopic examination   D. electroencephalogram
   E. psychometric examination

   3.____

4. The pathology of diabetes involves the FAILURE of the body to produce an adequate supply of
   A. sugar   B. carbohydrates   C. insulin
   D. salt   E. bile

   4.____

5. The one of the following statements that is TRUE about diabetes is that
   A. it can generally be cured if medical orders are followed
   B. it can generally be kept under control but not cured
   C. it is an infectious disease
   D. blindness is an inevitable result of it
   E. controlled diabetes is a progressively disabling disease

   5.____

6. Scurvy is caused by a deficiency of vitamin
   A. A   B. B   C. C   D. E   E. K

   6.____

7. Vitamin D deficiency is common because
   A. it can only be injected
   B. it is generally associated with poorly tasting foods
   C. only physicians can administer it
   D. it is not found naturally in many foods

   7.____

8. The one of the following vitamins that is used as an aid in coagulating blood is vitamin
   A. A   B. B   C. C   D. E   E. K

   8.____

19

9. The one of the following statements that is TRUE of Duchenne muscular dystrophy is that
   A. it is transmitted to the male children through the mother
   B. the male is the carrier of the disease
   C. the brain is primarily affected because of a lack of blood supply
   D. it is caused by a nutritional deficiency in the antepartum period
   E. only female children are susceptible to the disease

9.____

10. If a patient is repeatedly admitted to the hospital because of a series of mishaps in which he has suffered broken bones, the one of the following that is MOST likely to be true is that he is
    A. a rigid person   B. a diabetic   C. malingering
    D. accident prone   E. psychotic

10.____

11. The one of the following groups of illnesses that is known to be caused by bacteria is
    A. mental diseases   B. acute infectious diseases
    C. nutritional diseases   D. degenerative diseases
    E. cancerous tumors

11.____

12. The one of the following with which Hodgkin's Disease is COMMONLY associated is
    A. neurasthenia   B. meningitis   C. poliomyelitis
    D. cancer   E. tuberculosis

12.____

13. The one of the following diseases in which the determination of the sedimentation rate is IMPORTANT for diagnostic purposes is
    A. rheumatic heart disease   B. congenital heart disease
    C. hypertensive heart disease   D. diabetes
    E. gonorrhea

13.____

14. The one of the following disease classifications that would INCLUDE spinal meningitis is
    A. cancer or tumor   B. nutritional disease
    C. acute infectious disease   D. focal or local infection
    E. acute poisoning or intoxication

14.____

15. The one of the following diseases that may cause visual impairment and blindness is
    A. ringworm   B. osteomyelitis
    C. poliomyelitis   D. gall bladder disease
    E. diabetes

15.____

16. The one of the following that is NOT an anesthetic is
    A. cholesterol   B. nitrous oxide   C. sodium pentothal
    D. procaine   E. ethyl chloride

16.____

17. The one of the following that BEST describes the restrictions to be applied to   17.____
    Mr. K., a cardiac patient classified, according to the standards of the American
    Heart Association, as functional, Class IVD, is
    A. limited activity
    B. complete bed rest
    C. four hours rest daily
    D. prohibition of stair climbing, alcohol or tobacco
    E. convalescent status

18. Over time, geriatrics has become an increasingly important branch of medicine   18.____
    CHIEFLY due to
    A. greater specialization within the medical profession
    B. the discovery of penicillin and aureomycin
    C. advances in medical education
    D. increases in hospitalization
    E. the increase in the span of life

19. The one of the following which is MOST likely to be an occupational disease is   19.____
    A. cancer   B. cerebral hemorrhage
    C. septicemia   D. asthma
    E. nephritis

20. The one of the following that is a NUTRITIONAL disease is   20.____
    A. tuberculosis   B. scurvy   C. hepatitis
    D. lymphoma   E. scabies

21. Morbidity rate refers to the   21.____
    A. incidence of an illness
    B. ratio of births to deaths
    C. bacterial count
    D. degree of disability caused by an illness
    E. death rate

22. A pediatrician is a doctor who specializes in the treatment of   22.____
    A. children   B. foot diseases
    C. disabling illnesses   D. orthopedic diseases
    E. the aged

23. A sadistic person is one who   23.____
    A. receives gratification through suffering pain
    B. secures a great deal of satisfaction from his own body
    C. receives gratification from inflicting pain on others
    D. turns all feelings towards others back into his own personality
    E. seeks solace through deep mental depression

24. The one of the following which is said to be the masculine counterpart of the   24.____
    Electra Complex is the _____ complex.
    A. sexual perversion   B. frustration   C. Oedipus
    D. reanimation   E. repression

25. The one of the following conditions for which a patient would be admitted to a state mental hospital is
    A. schizophrenia
    B. muscular dystrophy
    C. pathological lying
    D. congenital syphilis
    E. psychoneurosis

    25.____

26. The one of the following statements which BEST describes the difference between a hallucination and a delusion is that
    A. hallucinations occur only at night
    B. delusions occur only with menopause
    C. delusions are primarily provoked by sexual function
    D. a hallucination has a basis in beliefs or ideas
    E. a delusion has a basis in beliefs or ideas

    26.____

27. Finger sucking in early childhood has long been a subject of discussion among psychiatrists.
    The one of the following statements that is GENERALLY accepted as true is that
    A. finger sucking denotes pending neuroses and the parents need psychiatric consultation
    B. finger sucking is a normal activity of early childhood and should not be interfered with
    C. finger sucking alters the child's facial contours and should be heavily discouraged
    D. finger sucking by a child over nine months old is due to emotional upset and needs treatment
    E. the physician should discuss possible remedial measures such as guards on fingers

    27.____

28. The one of the following who is said to be the *Father of Medicine* is
    A. Hippocrates   B. Pasteur   C. Galen
    D. Sydenham   E. Plato

    28.____

29. The one of the following who is credited with the improvement of conditions in mental hospitals and the founding of new ones in the United States is
    A. Andrew Jackson   B. Dorothea Dix
    C. William Knowlton   D. Robert Stack
    E. Rene Laennec

    29.____

30. The one of the following doctors whose name is COMMONLY associated with much of the early growth and subsequent progress of medical social work is Dr.
    A. Sigmund Freud   B. Richard C. Cabot
    C. Elizabeth Blackwell D. Carmyn Lombardo
    E. Thomas Parran

    30.____

KEY (CORRECT ANSWERS)

1.	A	11.	B	21.	A
2.	A	12.	D	22.	A
3.	D	13.	A	23.	C
4.	C	14.	C	24.	C
5.	B	15.	E	25.	A
6.	C	16.	A	26.	E
7.	D	17.	B	27.	B
8.	E	18.	E	28.	A
9.	A	19.	D	29.	B
10.	D	20.	B	30.	B

EXAMINATION SECTION
TEST 1

DIRECTIONS: Each question or incomplete statement is followed by several suggested answers or completions. Select the one that BEST answers the question or completes the statement. *PRINT THE LETTER OF THE CORRECT ANSWER IN THE SPACE AT THE RIGHT.*

1. A social worker meets with a refugee couple in the hospital soon after the birth of their son. The infant has Down's Syndrome and cardiac problems. The couple asks that the child be allowed to die. The social worker should FIRST:

    A. Report the case to child protective services because of the at-risk nature of the situation
    B. Offer the parents the option of relinquishing the child for adoption
    C. Encourage the parents to meet with other parents of Down's syndrome children
    D. Perform a bio-psychosocial assessment including cultural, religious and familial factors

2. The youngest child of a single mother with four children has been hospitalized for the second time in four months for lead poisoning. The doctor has refused to release the child back into an unsafe environment. During an interview with the hospital social worker, the woman says that the landlord refuses to have the apartment where she lives repainted and to make other necessary repairs. She would like to move, but she is unable to find affordable housing that will also allow four children. After reporting the situation to child welfare authorities, the BEST course of action for the social worker is to:

    A. advise the woman to withhold her rent until the repairs are made
    B. advocate for the child to be sent home since housing changes will be made soon
    C. assist the woman with locating resources for suitable housing
    D. report the landlord to the housing authority for his unwillingness to improve the property

3. An adolescent has been referred to a social worker because of school-related difficulties. During the intake session with the family, the parents become angry and begin verbally attacking the teen. The social worker's MOST appropriate action is to:

    A. allow the parents to continue to vent their anger
    B. stop the session and see the teen alone
    C. focus on the parents' expression of anger
    D. ask the teen to leave the room

4. A prolonged silence in an interview is MOST likely to:

    A. increase client discomfort
    B. ease the client's anxiety
    C. facilitate the social worker/client relationship
    D. assure the client of the social worker's attentiveness

5. During an interview with a social worker, a client begins to express suicidal ideation. What should the social worker's FIRST response be?

   A. Recommend hospitalization
   B. Assess the client's level of risk
   C. Establish a behavioral contract
   D. Provide supportive reassurance

6. A social worker maintains client records in a safe environment and only releases information as provided by law. The ethnical handling of client information is BEST described as protecting:

   A. the client's right of due process
   B. client confidentiality
   C. agency record requirements
   D. self-determination by the client

7. Social workers can BEST assess their own practice activities and results by:

   A. evaluating goal outcomes and positive behavioral changes in clients
   B. reviewing their personal performance evaluations
   C. keeping and reviewing case records and notes
   D. asking clients for anonymous evaluations

8. Delusions, hallucinations, and inappropriate affect are characteristic of:

   A. narcissistic personality
   B. anxiety disorders
   C. schizophrenia
   D. antisocial personality

9. In the social worker/client relationship, acceptance may BEST be defined as:

   A. a neutral stance
   B. unconditional positive regard
   C. agreement with client's values
   D. an expression of approval

10. A social worker who conducts personal safety seminars for senior citizens is engaging in what kind of activity?

    A. Social planning
    B. Community development
    C. Primary prevention
    D. Secondary prevention

11. A social worker consistently exceeds job standards. To help the social worker maintain this level of performance, the supervisor should:

    A. put a letter of commendation in the social worker's personnel file
    B. provide the social worker with feedback on an ongoing basis
    C. arrange a merit increase for the social worker
    D. recommend the social worker for promotion

12. A social worker is interviewing for the first time a 35-year-old woman who is extremely upset and depressed. Her husband has just moved out of the house, telling her that he wants a divorce. The couple has two teenage children. The social worker's primary task is to:

    A. facilitate a referral to a women's support group
    B. assess the impact of the situation on the children
    C. refer the client for legal advice
    D. help the client to define issues and set priorities

13. A teacher at a Head Start school discusses with a social worker a child who is poorly dressed, sleepy, and withdrawn. The social worker should FIRST:

    A. obtain psychological testing for the child
    B. report the child to child protective services
    C. assess the home situation
    D. refer the child for a physical examination

14. In working with a depressed client, the social worker's FIRST task is to:

    A. identify existing client support systems
    B. evaluate the need for hospitalization
    C. assess the client's level of risk
    D. refer for medication evaluation

15. A social worker from a rape crisis center has been called to an emergency room to assist with a rape victim. The social worker's PRIMARY role is to:

    A. assist law enforcement personnel in gathering information
    B. provide support and information to the rape survivor
    C. solicit support for the client from significant others
    D. obtain a comprehensive psychological assessment

16. An adolescent belongs to his high school honor society but rarely attends meetings or volunteers for projects. For the student, this club represents what kind of group?

    A. Natural
    B. Task
    C. Primary
    D. Reference

17. A client who was involuntarily admitted to an inpatient facility is uncooperative and refuses to give social history information to the social worker. The BEST option available to the social worker is to:

    A. encourage the client's expression of anger and resentment
    B. contact a family member to obtain the necessary information
    C. continue to pursue the needed information with the client
    D. delay completing the social history until the client has become cooperative

18. A mental health service unit is assessing families for treatment. A social worker, clinical psychologist, psychiatrist, and substance abuse counselor each evaluate the family members. Each staff member contributes information for treatment recommendations. In arriving at a treatment plan, which of the following terms BEST describes the model being used?

    A. Collaborative
    B. Interdisciplinary
    C. Consultative
    D. Consensus building

19. A social worker is meeting with the parents of an infant recently diagnosed with mental retardation. In the initial conference, the social worker should FIRST provide the parents with:

    A. names and locations of appropriate community educational resources
    B. factual information about the child's specific form of mental retardation
    C. an opportunity to discuss their feelings and ask relevant questions
    D. a referral to a support group for parents who are experiencing a similar situation

20. The wife of a physically abusive alcoholic calls the social worker for advice. In an angry, aggressive state, her husband had called her to say he was coming home to punish their nine-year-old daughter for the C she earned in history class. The social worker should recommend that the wife FIRST:

    A. call Alcoholics Anonymous or Alanon for assistance
    B. call the police for protection
    C. remove herself and daughter from the home
    D. send the daughter to a neighbor's house

21. When considering the formation of a support group, the social worker's FIRST step should be to:

    A. arrange for a location and time for group meetings
    B. substantiate the need for a group
    C. define the purpose of the group
    D. advertise the group and its purpose

22. In preparation for an annual performance evaluation, a supervisor will MOST effectively encourage the social worker's professional development by:

    A. allowing the worker to write a self-evaluation
    B. giving a written evaluation and allowing a written comment from the worker
    C. using both verbal and written processes throughout the evaluation period
    D. arranging for a peer review using group process

23. A 16-year-old adolescent with a history of acting out behaviors in school is referred to a social worker at a neighborhood outreach center. The adolescent is sullen and silent for the initial interview. In order to facilitate communication, the social worker's MOST appropriate action is to:

    A. ask the client to return when ready to talk
    B. contact the client's teacher to gather more information
    C. ask the client about the acting out behavior
    D. focus on the client's resentment about being referred

24. A school social worker is conducting a research project using a random sample of fourth grade students. By using a random sample, the social worker will be able to:

    A. control for intervening variables
    B. generalize results to this school's fourth grade population
    C. provide information on the needs of all fourth grade students
    D. demonstrate differences between low and high achievers

25. During an interview a client states that her husband has sexually molested their seven-year-old son in the past. She states that the molestation has stopped. The social worker should:

    A. schedule an interview with the entire family
    B. refer the child for individual therapy
    C. report the molestation to the authorities
    D. help the mother to deal with her feelings

KEY (CORRECT ANSWERS)

1.	D	11.	B
2.	C	12.	D
3.	C	13.	C
4.	A	14.	C
5.	B	15.	B
6.	B	16.	D
7.	A	17.	B
8.	C	18.	B
9.	B	19.	C
10.	C	20.	C

21. B
22. C
23. D
24. B
25. C

TEST 2

DIRECTIONS: Each question or incomplete statement is followed by several suggested answers or completions. Select the one that BEST answers the question or completes the statement. *PRINT THE LETTER OF THE CORRECT ANSWER IN THE SPACE AT THE RIGHT.*

1. A 12-year-old child has become unmanageable, according to the parents. The parents blame the child's behavior on the negative influence of the child's friends and have banned the friends from their home. The parents request help in changing their child's behavior. The BEST initial intervention by the social worker is to:

     A. confront the child immediately and strongly with the behavior
     B. interview the child to establish a rapport
     C. interview the child and the parents together and separately to define the problem
     D. educate the whole family on techniques for behavior management

1.___

2. A social worker at a community mental health agency is asked to attend an emergency meeting of employees from a paper mill. The employees have learned the mill will be closed at the end of the week, due to bankruptcy. What is the FIRST step the social worker should take in assisting the group?

     A. Collect demographic information
     B. Identify the perceived problems
     C. Arrange a meeting with management
     D. Find legal counsel for the group

2.___

3. A client who is HIV-positive has been unwilling to share this information with his sexual partner. The social worker has used various strategies in an attempt to bring the client to a point where he is willing for inform his partner of his medical condition. Unfortunately, all the strategies failed. Which of the following tasks should be given the highest priority?

     A. Respect the client's wishes and maintain confidentiality.
     B. Alert the client's partner to the potential lethal risk.
     C. Consult an attorney regarding the relevant statutes and case law.
     D. Start from the beginning, and try all the clinical strategies one more time.

3.___

4. An elderly client in good physical health is still withdrawn a year after the death of her husband. She is not communicative, is not sleeping well, and has lost a great deal of weight. After possible medical causes are ruled out, the MOST likely conclusion by the social worker is that she is experiencing:

     A. depression
     B. regression
     C. anxiety
     D. bereavement

4.___

5. Trust, mastery, and separation are tasks of which stage of individual development?

   A. Young adult
   B. Adolescence
   C. Infancy
   D. Pre-adolescence

6. A three-year-old child is enrolled in a preschool program. The child experiences episodes of crying and tantrums upon the mother's departure. This behavior is MOST often associated with:

   A. stranger anxiety
   B. immaturity
   C. separation anxiety
   D. school phobia

7. A hospital social worker received a referral to see an elderly widow who was admitted after she was found lying on the floor in her apartment. The widow was unkempt and disheveled and had left the stove on after making a meal. The social worker's FIRST action should be to:

   A. refer the client for home care services
   B. assess the client's self-care ability
   C. contact the client's next of kin
   D. refer the client to adult protective services

8. A client is admitted to a chemical dependency treatment facility following emergency treatment of an alcohol-related major physical problem. The client admits to drinking occasionally but spends most of the initial interview complaining about his boss. This is an example of what defense mechanism?

   A. Rationalization
   B. Reaction formation
   C. Denial
   D. Displacement

9. In an alcoholic family system, the child who assumes responsibility for care of the family is taking on the role of:

   A. scapegoat
   B. hero
   C. lost child
   D. mascot

10. An 87-year-old male living alone is being served by a community mental health care clinic. He has memory loss, does not recognize family members, and habitually wanders away from home. After assessment and establishment of guardianship, the social worker should NEXT explore:

    A. resources available within the client's family
    B. nursing home placement
    C. day care placement
    D. services to the aged in the community

11. A patient who is capable of informed consent chooses to discontinue services and the social worker does not interfere. The patient is exercising the right of:

    A. confidentiality
    B. self-determination
    C. termination
    D. disengagement

12. A client who has been in substance abuse treatment has obtained rental assistance. His future landlord calls the client's social worker for a reference. In response to the landlord's questions about any substance abuse history, the social worker should:

    A. answer the question directly as asked
    B. secure a release of information from the client
    C. avoid the question by redirecting conversation
    D. tell the landlord the information is confidential

13. The PRIMARY effect of empathy in casework relationships is to:

    A. give the client feedback about his or her behavior
    B. breakthrough barriers in thinking
    C. alleviate the client's suffering
    D. enhance the social worker-client relationship

14. The idea of people with differing values and lifestyles living in tolerance with each other is BEST described as:

    A. Cultural pluralism
    B. The melting pot concept
    C. Ethnocentrism
    D. Structural assimilation

15. A family has survived a natural disaster but has lost their home and all belongings. As a member of the Disaster Relief Team, a social worker should FIRST assist the family to:

    A. meet their primary needs
    B. file an insurance claim
    C. relocate
    D. obtain a support network

16. Which of the following is MOST likely associated with autism?

    A. Hearing impairment
    B. Impaired perceptions
    C. Failure to thrive
    D. Lack of social interaction

17. When a child must be placed outside of the birth family, the FIRST placement option a social worker needs to consider is:

    A. kinship networks
    B. friends of the family
    C. a foster family of the same ethnicity
    D. an adoptive family

18. The primary purpose of a service plan is to:

    A. evaluate client progress
    B. assess the home situation
    C. monitor behavioral changes
    D. establish goals

19. A client tells her social worker that a previous social worker had sex with her. The client does not name the former social worker. The social worker who is currently treating the woman should FIRST:

    A. educate the client about how to file an ethics complaint
    B. refer the client to a sexual abuse counselor
    C. refer the client to the police department
    D. investigate the identity of the first social worker

20. During an application interview with a social worker, a prospective client was deemed ineligible for assistance. The social worker should FIRST:

    A. advise the client of appeal procedures
    B. suggest the client seek support elsewhere
    C. recommend that the client obtain legal counsel
    D. arrange for a supervisor to validate the denial

21. A neurologist has referred a two-year-old child with cerebral palsy to an agency for evaluation and possibly early intervention. The agency's social worker should FIRST:

    A. engage the child in play as part of the assessment
    B. help the child's parents resolve issues of grief and loss
    C. begin working with the family to learn about their needs
    D. refer the child for a skills attainment evaluation

22. Socioeconomic status (SES) is an index which takes into account:

    A. status in the community
    B. credit rating
    C. work experience and income
    D. income, education and occupation

23. Which of the following communication techniques is LEAST likely to be used by the social worker in an initial interview?

    A. Questioning
    B. Listening
    C. Clarifying
    D. Disclosing

24. The major determinants of a client's motivation and ability to use social work services are the:

    A. socioeconomic class of the client and the ability to pay for services
    B. age of the client and the environmental factors supporting change
    C. client's hope that the situation can improve and the discomfort with the situation itself
    D. skill of the social worker and the client's acceptance of personal responsibility for actions

25. A social worker is providing services to a single mother who has low self-esteem and periodic depressive episodes. During one session the social worker observes that the client's six-year-old child has bruises on his upper arms. The mother cannot adequately explain them. The social worker should FIRST:

    A. suggest to the mother that the child be examined by a physician
    B. inform the mother that suspected child abuse must be reported
    C. talk with the child alone about the possibility of abuse
    D. discuss appropriate discipline methods with the mother

KEY (CORRECT ANSWERS)

1. C
2. B
3. C
4. A
5. A
6. C
7. B
8. C
9. B
10. A
11. B
12. D
13. D
14. A
15. A
16. D
17. A
18. D
19. A
20. A
21. C
22. D
23. D
24. C
25. B

EXAMINATION SECTION
TEST 1

DIRECTIONS: Each question or incomplete statement is followed by several suggested answers or completions. Select the one the BEST answers the question or completes the statement. *PRINT THE LETTER OF THE CORRECT ANSWER IN THE SPACE AT THE RIGHT.*

1. An adult client is seeking treatment at a community mental health clinic. For over a year, she has been overwhelmed with a sense of helplessness and feelings of intense fear, and has had difficulty in performing at work. During the intake interview, the client reports she was sexually abused as a child. According to the DSM-IV, the client would MOST likely be diagnosed as having which disorder?

    A. Major depressive
    B. Dysthymic
    C. Depersonalization
    D. Posttraumatic stress

1.____

2. A woman whose child was recently diagnosed with a terminal illness is referred to a hospital social worker. The woman tells the social worker that her child is not ill and will not need to see the doctor again. Which of the following defense mechanisms is represented by the mother's response?

    A. Rationalization
    B. Denial
    C. Displacement
    D. Intellectualization

2.____

3. A client who has received services for several years in a dialysis unit appears for a routine visit. The nurse notices that the client's affect is markedly different from the last visit. After ruling out compliance concerns, the nurse refers the client to the unit social worker. When seeing the social worker, the client seems detached, self-absorbed, and tearful. The social worker should FIRST:

    A. assess changes in the client's life situation
    B. schedule a family conference
    C. explore the client's concerns about dying
    D. discuss the client's feelings about dialysis

3.____

4. During the first appointment at a family agency, a mother is encouraged by the social worker to express her feelings about the recent placement of her child in a residential facility for the developmentally disabled. The client talks at length instead about her physical health problems. The social worker should FIRST:

    A. take a full developmental history on the child
    B. redirect the mother to the reasons for the child's placement
    C. evaluate the mother's focus on her own needs
    D. listen attentively to the mother as a way of building rapport

4.____

35

5. A social worker at a community mental health center is working with a 21-year-old client who has been experiencing a great deal of rejection from family and friends. The rejections followed an admission by the client that she is a lesbian. During the third session the client begins to cry and says *maybe my mom is right. She says all I need to do is find the right man*. After reflecting the client's unhappy feelings, the social worker should NEXT:

    A. use universalization to provide reassurance to the client about the behavior of others in these circumstances
    B. explore the client's psychosocial history to determine the origins of her sexual orientation
    C. encourage the client to spend some time rethinking her sexual orientation before continuing with the *coming out* process
    D. arrange for a family session to assist the client's family in understanding how to best support a gay family member

6. A social worker is asked to assist an elderly client in making alternative living arrangements. In the initial interview, the client repeatedly attempts to discuss past experiences. What is the social worker's MOST appropriate response to the client?

    A. Ignore the references to the past
    B. Facilitate discussion of the recollections
    C. Evaluate the client for dementia
    D. Redirect the focus to the living arrangements

7. A hospital social worker interviews a couple whose infant has recently been hospitalized for cystic fibrosis. The social worker notices that the parents are reluctant to touch the child. Based on this observation, the social worker's FIRST intervention should be to:

    A. have the parents talk about their reactions to the child's illness
    B. refer the couple to an appropriate support group
    C. evaluate the situation for out-of-home placement for the child
    D. provide the couple with information about cystic fibrosis

8. A client, diagnosed as borderline personality disorder, is verbalizing destructive thoughts directed at herself. While she does admit to depression, she denies any intention to act on the thoughts. The social worker should FIRST:

    A. seek in-patient hospitalization of the client
    B. explore with the client the basis of the depression
    C. complete a suicide risk assessment
    D. refer the client to a psychiatrist for medication

9. As part of the social work process, assessment is BEST described as a:

    A. discrete task to be completed before effective intervention can begin
    B. continuing process throughout the course of intervention
    C. way to measure the effectiveness of the intervention process
    D. method of setting the goals of the intervention process

10. Random error is assessed by:

    A. instrument reliability
    B. instrument validity
    C. external validity
    D. correlation

11. An 50-year-old client diagnosed with chronic alcoholism is at greatest risk for which of the following disorders?

    A. Parkinson's disease
    B. Alzheimer's disease
    C. Korsikoff's disease
    D. Senile dementia

12. A hospital social worker meets with three adult children of an elderly woman. The woman's physician has recommended discharge to a long-term care facility because she is unable to care for herself. The woman refuses this recommendation, and the children cannot agree on a plan. The social worker should FIRST:

    A. define the problem with the children
    B. develop a contract with the woman
    C. gather a social history from the children
    D. provide referrals to home care agencies

13. An adult client who is HIV positive and addicted to drugs and alcohol is receiving social work services from a local AIDS service organization. The client has responsibility for a young grandchild whose mother died of AIDS. The social worker suspects the child is the target of verbal abuse and possible neglect. Which assessment tool can BEST be used by the social worker to gain a better understanding of the situation?

    A. Genogram
    B. Sociogram
    C. Social network map
    D. Ecomap

14. A social worker employed with a public school system makes an initial home visit with a 15-year-old female client at the request of the client's probation officer. Before the social worker begins the assessment of the client and home situation, the client says *I don't have to tell you anything, and I won't tell you anything*. To facilitate the client's participation, the social worker's BEST response would be to tell her that:

    A. there are potential legal consequences for noncompliance
    B. she does indeed control whether she will cooperate
    C. her probation officer has requested the assessment
    D. the assessment is necessary in order to provide services

15. A social worker is interviewing the parents of an adolescent who has recently begun resisting their authority. The parents are angry and confused about how to handle the situation. When the social worker asks questions about other family members, the father says *You're not getting it; it is our son who is the problem*. The social worker should FIRST:

    A. recommend an individual assessment of the adolescent
    B. obtain a developmental history of the adolescent
    C. discuss the importance of understanding everyone's perspective
    D. redirect questions toward the adolescent's behavior

16. During the first interview in the home with a pregnant, unmarried 15-year-old and her mother, the teenager states firmly to the social worker that she wants to keep her baby. The mother asks the social worker to tell the daughter about how difficult it will be to care for the baby. The teenager states, *I don't want to be talked out of keeping my child*. The social worker's FIRST response should be to:

    A. provide the teenager with the positives and negatives of caring for an infant
    B. explore the mother's feelings about her daughter's pregnancy
    C. discuss the teenager's feelings about being forced into a decision
    D. facilitate communication between the mother and daughter

17. Which situation is an example of role reversal in a parent-child relationship?

    A. A seven-year-old girl repeatedly comforting and reassuring her distressed mother following a marital separation
    B. A nine-year-old girl sharing her mother's concerns about household bills
    C. A single mother expecting her 10-year-old son to stay at home unsupervised
    D. An 11-year-old boy demanding of his mother that his meals be on the table at a certain time and that his laundry be done

18. A client is concluding treatment at a family counseling agency. The client feels very appreciative of the social worker's services. At the end of the interview, the client offers a substantial monetary gift to the social worker in addition to paying the fee to the agency. The social worker should:

    A. accept the gift, acknowledging the client's contribution to treatment
    B. refuse the gift, basing the action on ethical standards of practice
    C. accept the money but with the understanding that it will be donated to a local charity
    D. refuse the personal gift and suggest that the client make a donation to the agency instead

19. During group therapy sessions, one of the members continuously blames others in the group for the depression and hopelessness the member experiences. In an effort to address the client's concerns, the social worker should FIRST:

    A. tell the client that these feelings stem from fears
    B. encourage the client to talk about feelings within the group
    C. reiterate the guidelines for the group process
    D. encourage the group to be more sensitive to the client's feelings

20. A child welfare worker is interviewing a parent who admits brutally abusing a child during a rage. On hearing the details, the social worker becomes very angry. To appropriately deal with the anger, the social worker should:

    A. acknowledge the anger to the parent and continue the interview
    B. ignore the anger and proceed with the interview
    C. recognize the anger and discuss it later with the supervisor
    D. request the case be transferred to another social worker

21. A false, fixed belief that is inconsistent with the intelligence and cultural background of the person holding the belief and held despite rational explanation and evidence to the contrary is BEST defined as a(n):

    A. denial
    B. illusion
    C. hallucination
    D. delusion

22. A social worker learns that a father becomes angry when his two-year-old son soils or wets his pants. The father's usual response to this behavior is to yell at the child to *grow up*. The father's behavior MOST likely reflects:

    A. dysfunctional relationship with the child
    B. a distorted perception of child development
    C. a need for developing new ways to cope with stress
    D. displacement of anger toward the other parent

23. In which instance is identifying information from an individual client's case record NOT appropriate for use?

    A. When the social worker is going on vacation, leaving another social worker in charge of the case
    B. When consulting with a professional to gain insight into the client's condition
    C. When agency data is being used for supporting grant proposals
    D. When the social worker is participating in clinical supervision

24. A woman in treatment with a social worker comments that whenever her adolescent son becomes angry, she feels as though she is a failure as a parent. The social worker comments that all adolescents become angry at times. The social worker's technique is known as:

    A. clarifying
    B. interpreting
    C. confronting
    D. normalizing

25. A new supervisor recently promoted from another part of the agency supervises a social worker who conducts group therapy with adolescent clients. In the new position, the supervisor often *drops in* on group sessions and interacts with clients. What is the FIRST step the social worker should take in dealing with this situation?

    A. Integrate the supervisor into group activities with the clients
    B. Talk with the supervisor about the impact of dropping in on groups
    C. Arrange a meeting with the agency director to clarify the supervisor's role
    D. Respect the supervisor's position and allow the supervisor to judge the situation

KEY (CORRECT ANSWERS)

1.	D	11.	C
2.	B	12.	A
3.	A	13.	D
4.	D	14.	B
5.	A	15.	C
6.	B	16.	C
7.	A	17.	A
8.	C	18.	B
9.	B	19.	B
10.	A	20.	C

21. D
22. B
23. C
24. D
25. B

TEST 2

DIRECTIONS: Each question or incomplete statement is followed by several suggested answers or completions. Select the one the BEST answers the question or completes the statement. *PRINT THE LETTER OF THE CORRECT ANSWER IN THE SPACE AT THE RIGHT.*

1. A client who has completed treatment and resolved the targeted problem is making excessive telephone calls to the social worker. The social worker should:

    A. inform the client that the therapeutic relationship is finished
    B. refer the client to another social worker in the agency
    C. limit the number of calls the social worker will accept
    D. schedule a session to determine any current problems

    1.____

2. In preparing a discharge summary, a social worker writes a case history describing the events leading up to the client's recent hospitalization. The history describes the assessment that was made and the exact symptoms that supported the assessment. The discharge summary was then placed in the client's record. The social worker's supervisor would consider this summary to be:

    A. incomplete because it did not describe what happened in treatment
    B. accurate in giving a complete account supporting admission
    C. satisfactory as a summary for use upon the client's readmission
    D. inappropriate because it contains the assessment

    2.____

3. A client states to a social worker that the social worker reminds him of his former fiancee and that he very much appreciates the social worker's caring for him. This is an example of:

    A. reaction formation
    B. idealization
    C. transference
    D. unconditional positive regard

    3.____

4. A client who is in therapy with a social worker has made significant progress over a period of three months. The client misses a scheduled appointment and does not return the social worker's calls. This behavior is MOST likely an indication of the client's:

    A. misunderstanding of the treatment contract
    B. negative transference in the therapeutic process
    C. establishment of satisfying relationships
    D. readiness for termination of treatment

    4.____

5. In an enmeshed family the children are LEAST likely to exhibit:

    A. role ambiguity
    B. respect for authority
    C. unclear boundaries
    D. difficulty in focusing

    5.____

6. A t-test is used to determine:

   A. causality
   B. standard deviation
   C. significance of differences between sample means
   D. significance at the .05 level of probability

7. A budgeting approach which categorizes expenditures and resources according to the agency's service areas is:

   A. zero-based
   B. program-based
   C. cost benefit
   D. line item

8. A married couple bring their six-year-old son in to see a social worker in private practice. The parents indicate the child recently began bedwetting after being toilet trained for three years. Upon questioning, the parents reveal the bedwetting began shortly after the parents brought their new baby home from the hospital. The six-year-old is MOST likely using the defense mechanism of:

   A. repression
   B. regression
   C. reaction formation
   D. displacement

9. A social worker may limit a client's right to self-determination when:

   A. agency policy requires the social worker to develop treatment plans that minimize liability for the agency
   B. in the social worker's professional opinion the client has made poor choices regarding treatment options
   C. there is pending legal action which would curtail the rights of the client to make decisions
   D. the client's actions or potential actions pose a serious and imminent risk to self or others

10. A social worker wants to develop insight into the ways the social worker's own attitudes and feelings affect relationships with clients. This understanding can be MOST effectively facilitated by a supervisor who promotes the use of:

    A. reflection
    B. analysis
    C. peer review
    D. problem assessment

11. At times a social worker may choose to use closed-ended questions to:

    A. permit the client to be in control
    B. provide needed structure and direction
    C. check out the client's ability to take the initiative
    D. challenge the client's point of view

12. A social worker who has mental health difficulties which interfere with professional judgment and performance should:

    A. continue to practice and engage in all regular activities but safeguard clients
    B. make a self-report on the situation to the state social work licensing board
    C. seek consultation and remedial action, which may include obtaining therapy and adjusting workloads
    D. continue to practice and use appropriate self-disclosure to assist clients to understand similar issues

13. To enhance a client's capacity to make decisions, the social worker should:

    A. analyze the situation for the client
    B. give the client written materials on decision making
    C. ask the client to make a decision independent of the social worker
    D. teach the client how to examine alternate solutions

14. A husband and wife both express to a social worker that their needs are not being met by the other. This situation described by the couple is BEST characterized by the absence of:

    A. boundaries
    B. homeostasis
    C. complementarity
    D. entropy

15. A mother, father, and 16-year-old daughter come to a social worker because the daughter is breaking curfew, running away from home, and failing in school. The mother states at the initial session that she does not know what to do and that they need help. After acknowledging the family's distress, the social worker should:

    A. establish the number of sessions the family is allowed with the social worker
    B. formulate goals for the family members
    C. clarify the parents' expectations of the social work intervention
    D. contract with the adolescent on specific behavior goals

16. A social worker is allowed to violate confidentiality if a client:

    A. initiates a lawsuit against the social worker
    B. is under the age of eighteen
    C. resides in a nursing home
    D. resists recommended social work intervention

17. A social worker faced with a practice situation that may pose an ethical dilemma should FIRST consult the:

    A. current supervisor
    B. social work licensing board'
    C. professional code of ethics
    D. most experienced colleague

18. Crisis intervention is a strategy which generally involves:

    A. having clients face their problems directly and come to terms with them
    B. acting on behalf of clients who cannot act for their own safety
    C. using chaining and sloping to change behaviors
    D. encouraging a high level of intensive activity by the client

19. When faced by a hostile client in an agency setting, it is BEST for the social worker to:

    A. suggest that the client's attitude is making the situation worse
    B. accept the client's hostility and redirect toward nonthreatening topics
    C. set limitations and structure for the interview session
    D. acknowledge the client's feelings and encourage discussion of them

20. If a client has a mood disorder that can be addressed within a limited time frame, the treatment approach of choice is:

    A. cognitive behavioral therapy
    B. crisis intervention
    C. insight-oriented psychotherapy
    D. client-centered therapy

21. A social worker is using a task-centered approach to provide services to a client. After completing an assessment on the client, the social worker's NEXT step should be to:

    A. develop a set of goals with the client
    B. redefine the relationship with the client
    C. outline tasks for the client
    D. monitor the client's progress in goal accomplishment

22. In therapy, a client describes herself as a failure because of repeated publisher rejections of her work. Although the client has a well-paying job and satisfying interpersonal relationships, she defines her identity in terms of her writing. In response to the woman's self-description, the social worker should FIRST:

    A. help the client be more realistic about her abilities
    B. determine if she uses writing to avoid other areas of her life
    C. encourage the client to find other outside interests
    D. further explore the client's feelings about being published

23. During an initial session with a social worker at a community mental health center, a self-referred adult client states, *I just need to let you know, I don't much like social workers*. The client adds that social workers *don't ever seem to be able to help anyone*. In order to facilitate the therapeutic process in this situation, the social worker should:

    A. point out to the client the discrepancy between the desire for services and the dislike of social workers
    B. reassure the client that it is safe to discuss any and all issues, problems, and concerns
    C. acknowledge that the client may have had bad experiences with social workers in the past
    D. encourage the client to explain how the stated view of social workers developed

24. A social worker conducts a home visit to a 45-year-old Latino client whose young son was killed in a recent automobile accident. The social worker observes that a large altar has been made, which contains many candles as well as pictures of the boy and other deceased relatives. The client sobs throughout the interview and tells the social worker that the boy has been communicating to the client nightly through angels. In order to most effectively work with the client, the social worker should FIRST:

    A. refer the client for a medical evaluation
    B. assess the client for psychotic symptoms
    C. explore mourning rituals of the client's family
    D. evaluate the potential of self-harm

25. A social worker is conducting an initial interview with a father and three teenage children. The mother died recently after a lengthy illness. Exploration indicates that the family members were not able to appropriately mourn the mother's death. To help them cope with the unresolved grief, the social worker should FIRST:

    A. encourage the family to discuss their loss
    B. obtain information about the mother's illness
    C. refer the family to a grief support group
    D. engage the family in structural family therapy

KEY (CORRECT ANSWERS)

1. D		11. B	
2. A		12. C	
3. C		13. D	
4. D		14. C	
5. B		15. C	
6. C		16. A	
7. B		17. C	
8. B		18. B	
9. D		19. D	
10. A		20. A	

21. A
22. D
23. D
24. C
25. A

EXAMINATION SECTION

TEST 1

DIRECTIONS: Each question or incomplete statement is followed by several suggested answers or completions. Select the one that BEST answers the question or completes the statement. *PRINT THE LETTER OF THE CORRECT ANSWER IN THE SPACE AT THE RIGHT.*

1. The one of the following which is the PRINCIPAL medium of casework service is
    A. skilled diagnosis and realistic treatment planning
    B. personal communication or relationship established between the client and the worker
    C. agency organization in relation to program objectives
    D. the combined knowledge, skill, and attitude of the worker

    1._____

2. Treatment aimed at helping the client maintain his adaptive pattern is directed toward
    A. alleviating undue pressures in the client's everyday life and strengthening his emotional reactions to psychological pressure
    B. modifying the client's unrealistic life pattern by confronting him with explanations for his behavior
    C. assuming a passive role in order to avoid disturbing the client's adjustment
    D. working with those aspects of the client's problems which are related to environmental factors

    2._____

3. On account of the multi-faceted and dynamic nature of clients' problems, of the following, it is NECESSARY for the social worker to
    A. analyze the total problem before proceeding with treatment
    B. develop a comprehensive treatment plan which approaches the main aspects of the total problem
    C. separate the personality and behavioral aspects of the problem from the social setting
    D. select some part of the problem as the unit for work

    3._____

4. The one of the following which is the MOST important consideration in evaluating the ego strength of an angry, deprived, mistreated, frustrated, evasive client is the client's ability to
    A. verbalize his problems to someone
    B. redirect his anger towards an object
    C. form a relationship with an accepting worker
    D. hold a job

    4._____

5. When a client is torn between choices that immobilize him or make his problem less manageable, the social worker should base his practice with the client on the following, with the EXCEPTION of
    A. identification of the client's problem
    B. persuading the client to act according to his instructions
    C. determination with the client of preferred approaches in dealing with the problem
    D. enabling the client to take constructive action to deal with the problem

6. Assume that a social worker reports that a mother with whom she is working claims that the school is discriminating against her children because she is a welfare recipient. Her children have a history of truancy and poor school achievement. The worker feels that the mother's assessment of the situation has some validity.
   Of the following, the BEST course of action for the worker to take is to
    A. support the mother's defense of her children and report the alleged discrimination by the school to the Board of Education
    B. inquire further into the reasons for the children's truancy and poor achievement with the children, the mother, and school officials
    C. explore with the mother her feelings about receiving public assistance, and encourage her to find a job so she won't need assistance
    D. disengage herself from her close involvement in this case since she has stopped being objective

7. A social worker has as a client a 17-year-old boy who is part of a group whose norm of behavior is cutting classes, frequent absenteeism, sexual promiscuity, and petty thievery. He wants to finish school and to grow up, but the present peer-group pressure militates against this, and he is damaging his values by following the group's norms.
   The social worker would be MOST helpful to this boy if, of the following, he takes the role of a
    A. mediator, to help support the boy against the demands of the group, and also to give him direct help in defending himself psychologically
    B. resource person, to refer the boy to a youth agency that would be able to work with the boy in his peer group
    C. interpreter, to help the boy realize the inappropriateness of his behavior in the peer group
    D. peer model, to help the boy identify with a young, successful person

8. A fifteen-year-old boy has been referred to a social worker with a history of arrests for repeated acts of minor delinquency, suspension from school for truancy, and a hostile attitude towards treatment. He is financially supported by his parents, but they seem to have stopped giving him emotional support and say that he is uncontrollable.
   The boy's interests would be served BEST if, of the following, the social worker's role were that of
   A. psychosocial counselor using traditional insight development
   B. educator in teaching the boy the skills he would need to succeed
   C. catalyst in family therapy, to help the boy and his parents handle their feelings and the reality problems constructively
   D. crisis intervenor, taking an assertive role to give direction and specific help

9. The one of the following which is a COMMON error made by new social workers who are beginning to find out about the influence of unconscious desires and emotions on human behavior is to
   A. probe the client unnecessarily
   B. become over-assured that they can solve the client's problem
   C. slow up the pace of the interview
   D. look for the proper treatment method based on the client's neuroses

10. Although we can judge statements about objective verifiable matters to be true or false, we are not similarly justified in passing judgment on subjective attitudes.
    Of the following, this statement BEST explains the rationale behind the social work principle of
    A. empathy   B. abreaction
    C. non-judgmentality   D. confidentiality

11. The one of the following which BEST describes the meaning of ambivalence in social work is: The
    A. social worker refrains from imposing his moral judgments on the client
    B. supervisor assists the worker in understanding the psychological causes for the client's behavior
    C. client is seeking someone who will understand the subjective reasons for his behavior
    D. client has conflicting interests, desires, and emotions

12. The CORRECT definition of the term *acceptance* as used in social work is as follows:
    A. A decision made at intake to accept the client as a case for the agency to handle
    B. The concept of a positive and active understanding by the worker of the feelings a client expresses through his behavior
    C. The concept that the worker does not pass judgment on the client's behavior
    D. Communication to the client that the worker does not condone and accept his antisocial behavior

13. Psychiatrists are usually concerned with the total functioning and integration of the human personality.
    Of the following, social workers USUALLY concentrate on
    A. the same thing but for shorter periods of time
    B. the same thing but without prescribing medication
    C. helping the client to deal with the presenting problem
    D. making the proper referrals to assist the client in dealing with his problem

14. The one of the following which is a DESCRIPTIVE term for a client who is resistive, breaks appointments, withholds information, beclouds issues, related to others in a primitive, often distorted fashion, and acts out his wishes and conflicts in his contact with the worker is
    A. psychotic
    B. manic depressive
    C. paranoid schizophrenic
    D. character disorder

15. The one of the following which is a MAJOR reason why it is so difficult for social workers to exert influence on social policy is:
    A. Social workers are trained to implement existing policies, not to change those that are unworkable
    B. Those who make policy are influenced by numerous forces, persons, values, and aspirations, not all of which relate directly to the policy decisions to be made
    C. As a result of the heavy concentration on casework in the graduate schools, most social workers put more emphasis on working with individuals, rather than on social policy
    D. Psychological and psychiatric concepts are disputed by experts in the field, so that it is difficult to diagnose motives

16. The one of the following which is the BEST explanation of the rationale of *crisis intervention* as a treatment method is:
    A. A little help, rationally directed and purposefully focused at an extremely critical time in the client's life, can be more effective than more extensive help given during a less critical period
    B. Because clients are more likely to react precipitously at times of crisis, social workers must give particular emphasis at such times to providing direct and aggressive advice and assistance
    C. The social worker should make full use of the client's vulnerable emotional state at a time of crisis in order to bring him face to face with his defense mechanisms and with the realities of life
    D. The client's urgent need for emotional support at times of crisis should be used by the social worker at such times to gain the client's confidence and trust

17. In establishing contact with a new, unfamiliar group, of the following, the group worker's usual FIRST action should be to
    A. discuss the sponsoring agency and its function
    B. give special attention to the less aggressive members
    C. reinforce the authority of the natural group leader
    D. approach the group at their own level of language and interests

18. If a group worker should become aware that some members of his group feel resentful toward him, of the following, it would GENERALLY be advisable for the worker to
    A. make a special effort to please the resentful members
    B. offer to resign from leadership of the group
    C. attempt to convey to the resentful members his own attitude of acceptance of them
    D. enlist the support of other group members to convince the resentful ones of his good intentions

19. Assume that, during the sixth weekly session of activity group therapy with a group of adolescent boys, they engage in horseplay, use obscene language, and become quite uncontrollable.
    Of the following, it can SAFELY be concluded that the
    A. boys are testing the worker to learn his limits of tolerance
    B. worker's status as the group leader is being seriously challenged
    C. composition of the group should be changed
    D. worker should end the session and dismiss the boys

20. Of the following, the role of the group worker at meetings of a group which has its own officers is to
    A. withdraw from the activities of the group
    B. make decisions for the group if required
    C. clarify issues and teach skills when necessary
    D. handle hostile or aggressive members

21. Schizophrenia in children USUALLY becomes manifest
    A. during the latency period
    B. during adolescence only
    C. when the mother has a history of schizophrenia
    D. during early childhood or adolescence

22. Sickle cell anemia is a blood disease MOST commonly found in children whose parents are
    A. Caucasian
    B. black or Latin American
    B. interracial
    D. oriental

23. A decline in hearing and vision takes place in healthy persons during the period BEGINNING at age
    A. 30   B. 40   C. 50   D. 60

24. The MOST common complaint made by psychiatric patients is concerned with
    A. depression   B. panic   C. insomnia   D. fatigue

25. The one of the following which is *most likely* to cause the reappearance in old age of a previously compensated neurosis is
    A. decrease in social status, loss of persons and possessions or presence of injuries and illnesses
    B. decrease in sensory and cognitive capacities resulting in poor reality testing
    C. cerebro-arteriosclerosis or other cerebrovascular disturbance
    D. decrease in financial resources, resulting in heightened anxiety

25._____

KEY (CORRECT ANSWERS)

1. B
2. A
3. D
4. C
5. B

6. B
7. A
8. C
9. A
10. C

11. D
12. B
13. C
14. D
15. B

16. A
17. D
18. C
19. A
20. C

21. D
22. C
23. B
24. A
25. A

TEST 2

DIRECTIONS: Each question or incomplete statement is followed by several suggested answers or completions. Select the one that BEST answers the question or completes the statement. *PRINT THE LETTER OF THE CORRECT ANSWER IN THE SPACE AT THE RIGHT.*

1. Of the following, group approaches are COMMONLY used for
    A. encounter, discussion, training, and administration
    B. education, counseling, therapy, and recreation
    C. counseling, recreation, catharsis, and crisis intervention
    D. counseling, leadership, administration, and training

    1._____

2. The purposes of group counseling are the following, with the EXCEPTION of
    A. avoidance of treating pathology as such
    B. helping clients attain a better level of functioning
    C. modifying social and familial problems
    D. resolving intra-psychic conflicts

    2._____

3. The separation of public assistance recipients into categories had its origins in the
    A. Elizabethan poor law
    B. numerous amendments to the Social Security Act
    C. legislation of the Massachusetts Bay Colony
    D. Social Security Act of 1935

    3._____

4. The one of the following which is the FIRST form of social insurance to be widely developed in the United States is
    A. workmen's compensation or industrial accident insurance
    B. unemployment insurance programs
    C. temporary disability insurance
    D. old age insurance for industrial workers

    4._____

5. The doctrine of less eligibility, which has been considered over the years as a policy for public assistance programs, means most nearly that
    A. grants should always be below subsistence level in order to give recipients an incentive to seek employment
    B. eligibility for public assistance should be established on the basis of a limited number of basic budgetary needs
    C. income derived from public assistance benefits should not exceed the amount earned by the lowest paid independent worker in the community
    D. categories of need should be established in each community and ranked in order of priority in order to determine eligibility for assistance

    5._____

53

6. Social insurance programs such as OASDHI and unemployment insurance have been CRITICIZED widely because, of the following,
    a. there is an inherent conflict between the intent to prevent poverty on the one hand, and wage-relatedness of the programs on the other
    b. there is no relationship between the amount or the benefits and differences in cost of living in various localities within a state
    c. the programs do not include review of personal and family problems
    d. a large percentage of the grants go to persons who are otherwise financially able to support themselves

6._____

7. The one of the following which would be the basis of a family allowance plan SIMILAR to programs in effect in Canada and France is:
    a. Family size, for all needy families with minor children whose current annual income is below specified levels
    b. The total number of persons in the household, including all adults except those receiving social security benefits
    c. The number of minor children, available to all families and requiring no means test
    d. Income level, available to all families with minor children

7._____

8. A MAJOR criticism of social and health programs as they exist today has been the tendency towards a *problem focus* rather than a *social goals* approach.
    Of the following, this approach has resulted in
    a. a lack of an integrated, systematic development of programs that deal adequately with social and health problems
    b. excessive expenditures for the social and health problems that have received the most attention, at the expense of other equally serious problems
    c. a federal and nationwide approach rather than the more desirable *geographic approach*, which would bring delivery of services closer to the people
    d. the development of legislation which shows little evidence of recognition of the contributions that could be made by social planners

8._____

9. A striking feature of American culture is its tendency to identify standards of personal excellence with competitive occupational achievement.
    The one of the following which is the CONSEQUENCE of this feature for those unable to make one's own living through work is to
    a. increase incentive to find a productive job
    b. lower the individual's feeling of self-worth and generate a feeling of powerlessness
    c. give the individual a need to control the environment
    d. encourage increased educational attainment

9._____

3 (#2)

10. Of the following, the objectives and curriculum content of graduate schools of social work today GENERALLY indicate an *increased* emphasis on
    a. prevention and institutional change in addition to treatment
    b. knowledge of individual personality factors and treatment methods
    c. the separate methods and goals of classroom study and field work
    d. the use of the one-to-one instructor-student relationship for both classroom study and field work

10._____

11. At present, there is a general consensus among social welfare educators and administrators that not every job requires a professional social worker with a master's degree in social work.
    The one of the following which is the MOST important reason for this viewpoint is that personnel with lower educational qualifications can
    a. be used as a valuable temporary expedient for jobs that would otherwise remain unfilled
    b. perform certain social work tasks as well or even better than workers with master's degrees
    c. gain experience that will spur them on to attend a graduate school of social work in order to obtain the degree
    d. be used to reduce substantially personnel costs in public and private social work agencies

11._____

12. In an era of rapid change, of the following, the REAL test of the social work profession is to
    a. meet constructively the demands of that change
    b. hold to its traditional practices
    c. abandon its methods for new approaches
    d. wait to see what happens to other professions

12._____

13. The psychologist who is USUALLY associated with a theory of self-psychology which has as its basic concept the assertion that a man has a tendency to actualize himself, i.e., to maintain and improve himself, is
    A. Karl Jung   B. Sigmund Freud
    C. B.F. Skinner   D. Carl Rogers

13._____

14. Of the types of mental breakdown listed below, the disorder that ordinarily occurs at the MOST advanced age is
    A. cerebral arteriosclerosis
    B. neurasthenia
    C. dementia praecox
    D. paresis

14._____

15. Principles of crisis intervention in social casework have been derived LARGELY from the theoretical formulations of
    a. Harry Stack Sullivan and Clara Thompson
    b. August P. Hollingshead and Frederick C. Redlich
    c. Otto Rank and Jessie Taft
    d. Erich Lindemann and Gerald Caplan

15._____

16. Of the following, the MOST important reason that those responsible for the care of a child in placement should *never* depreciate the child's natural parents or the home from which he came is that the
    a. child's self-esteem depends on how he feels about his natural parents and his previous experiences
    b. natural parents may have been incapable of being adequate parents
    c. child may feel the substitute parents are jealous of his natural parents
    d. child will be forced into the position of defending his natural parents and will resent the substitute parents

17. Although day care was originally established mainly as a social service for working mothers, it has been found that, of the following,
    a. working mothers of physically and mentally handicapped children do not benefit from day care facilities
    b. most working mothers would prefer to leave their children with friends or relatives rather than at a day care center
    c. it would be economically feasible and beneficial for communities to establish day care centers which would be available to all mothers in the community
    d. day care can also be an educational experience for a child and be helpful in the development of peer relationships

18. Research studies of language development in young children have shown that, of the following,
    a. the multiple mothering of children in a large family retards language development
    b. language retardation in otherwise normal children is usually related to inadequate language stimulation
    c. language retardation is always associated with slow motor development
    d. children are usually slow in learning to talk when more than one language is spoken in the home

19. The *battered child syndrome* is reported to be one of the most difficult problems facing health officials. When a worker knows of a case of a child being severely physically abused, of the following, he SHOULD
    a. get psychiatric consultation to understand the parents' motives
    b. advise the child to stay away from the parents
    c. help the parents to see what they're doing is wrong
    d. report the case to child protective authorities

20. The one of the following which is a *psychological principle* which can BEST be described as a situation in which an individual experiences some ambivalence and indecisiveness in choosing one or more desired objects or goals is
    A. task-orientation   B. conflict
    C. apathy   D. projection

21. The *treatment method* which allows or encourages the client to express his charged feelings around a pressing emotional need is known as
    A. exploring
    B. synthesizing
    C. catharsis
    D. ventilating

22. The *emotional release* that results from recall of a previously forgotten painful experience is known as
    A. introjection
    B. abreaction
    C. sublimation
    D. free association

23. The *action* whereby an individual directs his aggression against an innocent bystander rather than expressing it against the source of his difficulties, is called
    A. displacement
    B. projection
    C. introjection
    D. abreaction

24. An *attempt* to attribute emotionally caused behavior to reasonable factors MORE acceptable to the individual is known as
    A. projection
    B. rationalization
    C. introjection
    D. free association

25. The UNCONSCIOUS *application* of elements of the experiences in a former relationship to a new relationship is known as
    A. projection
    B. abreaction
    C. transference
    D. sublimation

KEY (CORRECT ANSWERS)

1. B	11. B
2. D	12. A
3. A	13. D
4. A	14. A
5. C	15. D
6. A	16. A
7. C	17. D
8. A	18. B
9. B	19. D
10. A	20. B

21. D
22. B
23. A
24. B
25. C

EXAMINATION SECTION
TEST 1

DIRECTIONS: Each question or incomplete statement is followed by several suggested answers or completions. Select the one that BEST answers the question or completes the statement. PRINT THE LETTER OF THE CORRECT ANSWER IN THE SPACE AT THE RIGHT.

1. As a worker in the out-patient clinic, you are helping a patient complete a Medicaid application. Although he appears to be eligible, the patient is reluctant to give the information necessary to complete the application.
   Of the following, your MOST appropriate action in this situation would be to

   A. inform your supervisor that the patient is uncooperative and request permission to close the case
   B. advise the patient that he can not be seen in the clinic again unless the application is completed
   C. discuss with the patient the reasons for his reluctance to apply for medical assistance
   D. explain to the patient that the bill will be turned over to a collection agency if the Medicaid application is not completed

2. You are interviewing a middle-aged man who is depressed about having to be in the hospital for a medical emergency at this particular time, when his wife and children are away. You once had a similar personal experience, and managed to handle your feelings of loneliness and depression successfully.
   When the man finishes his story, which one of the following would be your most appropriate FIRST response?

   A. Tell the man how you handled your situation and suggest that he use the same approach
   B. Tell the man you know just how he feels and are sympathetic
   C. Suggest that, if he gets a good night's sleep, he will feel better in the morning
   D. Tell the man how you handled your situation, and explore with him his feelings about trying the same approach

3. As a worker on the pediatric service, you receive a phone call from a woman who reports that her neighbor's six-month-old infant has black and blue marks all over its body. She states that she has heard sounds from the neighbor's apartment that make her suspect the child has been beaten.
   Of the following, your MOST appropriate response to this call would be to

   A. refer the woman to central registry of special services for children, explaining that the agency will investigate and that her report will be confidential
   B. advise the woman that you cannot take action on the basis of a phone call but that she should come in to see you personally about the matter
   C. inform the woman that it is poor practice to become involved in the domestic affairs of neighbors
   D. tell the woman to contact the police and have the parents investigated and possibly arrested for child abuse

4. You have been counseling a long-term patient once a week for several weeks. However, due to a reorganization in your hospital's department of social work, this patient will be assigned to another worker within three weeks. Of the following, the MOST appropriate time to tell the patient about the change in workers is

   A. immediately to give you time to help the patient adjust to the idea of another worker
   B. at the time of the new worker's first visit,to avoid any possible resentment by the patient towards you
   C. at the beginning of your final visit, to allow time to tell the patient what you know about the new worker
   D. at the end of your final visit, to avoid a possible sentimental farewell scene

5. As a worker assigned to the psychiatric walk-in-clinic, you receive a phone call from a man who says that his wife has just swallowed 20 sleeping pills, after an argument. Of the following, your MOST appropriate action would be to

   A. advise the man to calm down because this is probably not a lethal dose
   B. tell the man to give his wife large quantities of black coffee and walk her around so that she does not become unconscious
   C. offer the man an emergency appointment in the marital counseling clinic
   D. instruct the man to get immediate emergency medical assistance for his wife

6. As you enter the clinic area where you are assigned as a worker, you see an elderly man trip and fall on the curb near the doorway. Which one of the following actions should you take FIRST?

   A. Inform the executive director about this accident
   B. Assist the man to his feet and help him into the clinic area so that he can be more comfortable
   C. Stay with the man and tell him not to move while you ask someone to summon help
   D. Go to the nearest phone and call the police

7. Assume that a client is telling you the details of her previous surgery, including her problems during after-care treatment and the reactions of her family members towards her treatment. Since she will shortly undergo another similar operation, she is anxious to avoid some of the problems she had the last time.
The number of written notes you should take while this patient is talking should be

   A. *extensive,* due to the considerable detail and complexity of the discussion
   B. *minimal,* since this discussion demands your full attention, and notes can be written after the interview
   C. *extensive,* so that the client will feel that her problems are of extreme importance
   D. *minimal,* since complete notes should be taken immediately after this discussion but before ending the interview

8. You are interviewing a patient for the second time and you find that your relationship with him is becoming rather strained, *which* of the following would be the BEST way to handle this situation? Consider this development to be

   A. *routine,* and review your own attitudes and actions towards the client during your first interview, and the content of the interview
   B. *unusual,* and analyze the client's personality for reasons for the negative reaction
   C. *routine,* and ask your supervisor to assign this case to another worker
   D. *unusual,* and ask the client to explain possible reasons for his hostility

9. Mrs. Heeney, a 58-year-old former out-patient of the diabetic clinic, was doing well with the use of oral medication for several years, but has required daily injectitons of insulin during the past year. However, she finds It difficult to give herself injections, despite instruction at the clinic, and as a result has been hospitalized for diabetic shock for the second time. The doctors ask you to see what can be done to help Mrs. Heeney. Of the following, your *FIRST* action should be to

    A. schedule a psychiatric evaluation and recommend therapy to help Mrs. Heeney overcome her fears
    B. talk with Mr. Heeney to see whether he would be willing to give his wife the daily injections
    C. tell Mrs. Heeney she will be kept in the hospital until she learns and is able to give herself the injections
    D. enlist Mrs. Heeney's cooperation in learning to give herself injections in the hospital and then at home with the help of a visiting nurse

10. Mrs. Dean, a waitress, age 24, has been seen in the Emergency Room for the second time in ten days as a result of on-the-job accidents. She has told the doctor that she is tired and tense all the time and is unable to concentrate on what she is doing at her job. The doctor has referred her to both the medical clinic and social services for further work-ups.
    As the worker assigned to this case, of the following, the *most* advisable way to handle this case *INITIALLY* would be to

    A. ask for a report on the completed medical work-up before interviewing Mrs. Dean, in order to be aware of any medical conditions which might be affecting her fatigue and tenseness
    B. interview Mrs. Dean during the period in which she is underoing the medical work-up, in order to determine whether there are any psycho-social factors contributing to her condition
    C. interview Mrs. Dean during the period in which she is undergoing the medical work-up, and recommend psychiatric consultation at the same time
    D. refer Mrs. Dean for a psychological evaluation, and schedule your preliminary interview after you have received a report on the evaluation

11. The clinic doctor has asked you to speak with Ms. Farley because she frequently breaks clinic appointments, which the doctor considers dangerous in light of her serious medical condition. During the Interview, you find that Ms. Farley seems to be more concerned about her housing and welfare problems than her medical condition.
    Of the following, the *BEST* way to handle this situation would be to

    A. tell Ms. Farley to discuss her housing and welfare problems directly with those agencies, because it is more important for the hospital social worker to help her with her medical problems
    B. tell Ms. Farley that you would like to help her with these other matters, but you think her health and medical care are of primary importance and should come first
    C. explore with Ms. Farley the nature and extent of her housing and welfare problems in order to see how you can be of help to her, deferring immediate discussion of her broken appointments
    D. tell her you will be glad to discuss her other problems with her, but only after you have first worked out and settled the matter of her broken medical appointments

12. You are asked to look into the case of William T., age 9, who was referred to the pediatric clinic by his school principal because he is inattentive and falls asleep in class. The pediatrician finds no medical basis for these problems. As the result of a home visit, you find that there is continual quarreling between his parents, which is having a bad effect on William and his two younger brothers. The father has been unemployed for six months.
Of the following, your BEST course of action would be to

    A. refer the case to special services for children as a suspected case of child neglect
    B. seek to place William T. and his brothers in a foster home until the parents can resolve their problems
    C. offer to help Mr. T. get a job and consider the possibility of obtaining a second medical opinion regarding William's inattentiveness and sleepiness
    D. ask your supervisor to consider whether the social worker should be assigned to make a fuller intra-familial assessment of this case

13. Mrs. Ware is the sole support of herself and her 9-year-old son, who is hospitalized for an orthopedic condition which requires a body cast from chest to ankles. The child will be ready to be discharged in two weeks, but will have to remain in the case for another three months and visit the clinic weekly. The ward team has asked you to see Mrs. Ware in order to plan for the discharge.
Of the following, the MOST appropriate way to advise Mrs. Ware during this interview would be to

    A. recommend that she take her vacation time or a leave of absence in order to care for her child
    B. suggest that the best thing she can do is place her son in a rehabilitation center so that she can go on working
    C. tell her that she should quit her job and go on unemployment insurance until her son is out of the cast
    D. work with her to help her arrive at what she feels would be best for both herself and her child

14. Ronald P., age 5, has a chronic condition for which he receives oral medication to be taken 4 times daily. Although this medication is effective in 90% of known cases, Ronald is usually out of control and requires emergency room care at least once a week. Mrs. P. says Ronald is given his medication regularly. However, during your discussion with the doctor on this case, he questions Mrs. P's reliability in giving Ronald the medication.
Of the following, the BEST way for you to handle this situation initially would be to

    A. have Mrs. P. keep a daily record of when she gives Ronald the medication and return this record to you in two weeks
    B. discuss this problem with the boy's father and ask him to make sure that the child is getting the medication regularly
    C. interview Mr. and Mrs. P. together at home, so that you can evaluate the family situation and any other factors which may relate to this problem
    D. suggest to the doctor that Ronald be hospitalized for a suitable period of time in order to determine definitely whether he can be controlled with regular medication

15. Mrs. Jurado's husband has been a patient on the medical ward for a week. Visiting hours are from 2-4 p.m. and 7-8 p.m. Mrs. Jurado comes daily shortly before 4 p.m. and usually leaves about 5:30 p.m. The nurses have been flexible but cannot continue to allow this, and ask you, the worker on the ward, to talk to Mrs. Jurado.
Of the following, you should ask the nurses to

    A. continue to be flexible about visiting hours with Mrs. Jurado, since it would be difficult to make her understand hospital policy.
    B. remain Mrs. flexible a day or two longer, until you help Jurado understand hospital policy on visiting hours
    C. restrict Mrs. Jurado to regular visiting hours, and let you know if she refuses, so that you can talk to her at that time
    D. restrict Mrs. Jurado to regular hours and explain the reasons to her themselves, since enforcing visiting hours is their responsibility

16. Which one of the following health service systems would generally be suitable for a chronically ill or disabled patient who has had an acute episode or a relapse at home?

    A. Skilled nursing home
    B. General hospital
    C. Extended care facility
    D. Home attendant service

17. Assume that you are trying to arrange placement for an elderly patient who, upon discharge from the hospital, will be able to get around and manage by herself, but will require some supervision.
Of the following, the MOST appropriate placement for this patient would be in a

    A. nursing home
    B. rehabilitation center
    C. chronic care facility
    D. health-related facility

18. Assume that one of your clients, a married woman with two small children, is in the hospital for a serious operation that will require a long-term stay. Her husband is regularly employed during the day.
Of the following, the MOST appropriate arrangement for care of this couple's children would be

    A. a foster home
    B. day care service
    C. homemaker service
    D. group home placement

19. Assume that you are helping an elderly patient with discharge planning. This patient, who is expected to live alone in his own apartment, will need around-the-clock assistance with personal needs, such as bathing and taking of medication.
Of the following services, the ONE that should be recommended for this patient is a

    A. homemaker
    B. housekeeper
    C. home attendant
    D. visiting nurse

20. The type of residence which provides an interim living and working experience in the transition from psychiatric hospital care to return to the community is commonly known as a

    A. rehabilitation center
    B. halfway house
    C. psychiatric clinic
    D. temporary day care facility

KEY (CORRECT ANSWERS)

1.	C	11.	C
2.	D	12.	D
3.	A	13.	D
4.	A	14.	D
5.	D	15.	B
6.	C	16.	B
7.	B	17.	D
8.	A	18.	C
9.	D	19.	C
10.	B	20.	B

———

TEST 2

DIRECTIONS: Each question or incomplete statement is followed by several suggested answers or completions. Select the one that *BEST* answers the question or completes the statement. *PRINT THE LETTER OF THE CORRECT ANSWER IN THE SPACE AT THE RIGHT.*

1. During an interview, you learn that a patient needs services from another agency. Of the following, the BEST way to make a referral for services from this agency is to   1.____

    A. call the agency to advise them that you are referring your client for services
    B. instruct the client to contact the agency and have the client fill out the required forms in advance
    C. write a referral letter to the agency explaining the client's problems and needs, and have the client bring it to the agency
    D. send the agency a release of information signed by the client and a summary of the client's problems, and request an appointment for the client

2. You are counselling an elderly woman who lives alone. You and the doctor have decided that she requires nursing home placement upon discharge from the hospital. However, the woman has expressed fear and concern about being uprooted from her home and living among strangers.   2.____
In this situation, the BEST of the following courses of action would be to

    A. try to convince the woman that a nursing home is best
    B. allow the woman to make her own decision, after offering her advice and guidance
    C. recommend that the woman be permitted to live in her own home and manage as best she can
    D. ask the woman's doctor to encourage her to accept nursing home placement

3. You are counselling Mrs. Andujar, a Spanish-speaking woman with limited ability to speak English, who was told by the pediatrician that no medical reason has been found for her child's abnormal behavior, and was referred to the child psychiatric clinic. However, after a month, Mrs. Andujar tells you that the child's behavior is worse and that she still doesn't have an appointment at the child psychiatric clinic. You discover that Mrs. Andujar has not returned the forms sent to her by the clinic.   3.____
Of the following, the BEST way to handle this situation is to

    A. tell Mrs. Andujar that nothing can be done until she completes the forms and returns them to the clinic
    B. send Mrs. Andujar to the clinic to explain her predicament to the social worker on that service
    C. help Mrs. Andujar complete the forms and ask the psychiatric clinic social worker to suggest the best way to expedite an appointment
    D. tell the pediatrician about Mrs. Andujar's difficulty with the forms as well as the child's condition and ask him to insist on an immediate clinic appointment

4. Arleen, age 7, has recovered from her illness and will soon be discharged from the hospital. She has had many difficult experiences in her young life. Her father deserted the family last year, and her mother, with whom she was very close, died six months ago. Since then, Arleen has been living with her grandmother, who is elderly and ill, and cannot continue to care for her. You and the grandmother have decided together that foster   4.____

home placement is essential for Arleen's well being, A referral has been accepted by special services for Children, and placement is anticipated in about two weeks. According to good social work practice, of the following, it would be MOST appropriate for you to

- A. ask Arleen whether she would be willing to live apart from her grandmother in a nice new home
- B. inform Arleen that she will be going to a nice home where she will be happy and have many new friends
- C. tell Arleen, with the participation of her grandmother, of the plan for placement and the reasons for it, giving her every opportunity to express her feelings
- D. advise Arleen of the plan for placement and the reasons for it, encouraging her to be brave no matter how sad she feels living apart from her grandmother

Questions 5-7.

DIRECTIONS: Answer Questions 5 through 7 based on the information given in the following case record.

Laura Jackson
Age: 52
Single
Parents: Deceased
Siblings: Sister – Sally Mays, age 53, married
Diagnosis: Multiple Sclerosis

Ms. Jackson, a high school graduate, supported herself as a sales clerk since graduation, but continued to live at home with her parents until their sudden death in an automobile accident 13 years ago. Since that time, she lived alone, but had continual contact with her older sister, Mrs. Sally Mays. A year ago, Ms. Jackson's hand became too unsteady for her to work. This condition had been preceded by forgetfulness and frequent mistakes. Examinations resulted in a diagnosis of multiple sclerosis and she became increasingly incapacitated until she had difficulty feeding and dressing herself. After a very serious fall, Ms. Jackson was hospitalized. The case worker, together with Mrs. Mays, arranged for Ms. Jackson to be placed in a nursing home in anticipation of her discharge from the hospital. She would be unable to care for herself alone at home, and her sister could not take care of her, because of household responsibilities. Ms. Jackson is extremely unhappy and angry when she is told about the decision to place her in a nursing home. She accuses her sister of plotting to put her away. Mrs. Mays turns to the case worker for advice.

5. On the basis of the information given above, of the following, the circumstance which would help explain Ms. Jackson's anger when she was told about being placed in a nursing home is that she

    - A. is probably becoming paranoid as a result of her illness
    - B. has undoubtedly actively disliked her sister for years
    - C. was not involved in the process of making the decision
    - D. was a dependent person before she became ill

6. When Mrs. Mays turns to the case worker for advice after recognizing her sister's anger, of the following, it would be MOST appropriate for the case worker to FIRST

    - A. *reassure* Mrs. Mays that she has made the best decision for Ms. Jackson's care
    - B. *tell* Mrs. Mays that you will visit Ms, Jackson and calm her down

C. *help* Mrs. Mays to understand why Ms. Jackson is upset
D. *ask* Mrs. Mays to visit Ms. Jackson and explain why the decision was made

7. Of the following, the *MOST* important factor to consider in finding a nursing home for Ms. Jackson is 7.____

   A. the ratio of men to women among the patients
   B. a location that will make it possible for Mrs. Mays to visit frequently
   C. her need for a single room, since she has always lived alone
   D. the average age of the other patients

Questions 8-10.

DIRECTIONS: Answer Questions 8 through 10 based on the information given in the following case record.

Joan Drew
Age: 40
Single
Children: Tom 8, Rose 6
Diagnosis: Paralysis of entire left side due to a stroke Ms. Drew, who dropped out of school in the eleventh grade, has had a variety of jobs in factories, as an elevator operator, and as a domestic. She now receives public assistance. In June, 2016, she was operated on for removal of her right kidney and for a hysterectomy. In November, 2017, she had a cerebro-vascular accident; diagnosis: hemiparesis left. In January, 2018, she had a cystoscopy operation.
After discharge in November, 2018, Ms. Drew was scheduled for weekly visits to the hospital's physical therapy clinic for treatment of her paralysis. To date she has continued her therapy faithfully and is now able to walk with a cane. However, her left hand and part of her arm have not responded well to treatment.
Ms. Drew's attitude is poor when she discusses her situation with the case worker. She feels that she will never recover because she is being punished for past wrong-doing. At times she feels persecuted by her doctors and others. She worries about her children; this appears to be unfounded, as they are healthy and doing well in school.

8. Ms. Drew's medical problems are described above in terms that would be used in a medical report. Of the following, the *MOST* important reason why the case worker should understand the meaning of these terms is to 8.____

   A. make it possible for doctors to include you in discussions of the patient
   B. improve your understanding of the patient's symptoms
   C. help you to sound like a professional at interdisciplinary meetings
   D. help your prospects for advancement in the medical social work field

9. The case worker should understand that Ms. Drew's fear that she is being punished for past wrong-doing is a problem that should be 9.____

   A. discussed with the supervisor for possible referral for psychiatric evaluation
   B. handled by psychiatric treatment
   C. treated by strong reassurance that she is not being punished for her sins
   D. considered to be an indication of psychotic behavior

10. Of the following, the underlying reason for Ms, Drew's exaggerated concerns about her children are probably the result of

    A. her fears about her own health and her future ability to care for her children
    B. her realization that she has made serious mistakes in bringing her children up
    C. her dependence upon her children to give her a sense of self-worth
    D. her desire to give her children more advantages and comforts than she had

Questions 11-14.

DIRECTIONS: Answer Questions 11 through 14 based SOLELY on the formation contained in the following passage.

After conducting and completing an interview, the interviewer is faced with the responsibility of recording it in some manner. Very considerable amounts of staff time and agency finances are absorbed in recording. Time and cost studies of agency expenditures indicate that, for every dollar spent on interviewing, three dollars are spent on recording. In addition to actual time spent by the worker in recording, such expense involves clerical transcribing time, filing time and space, and time in reading records.

Recording insures a continuity of client-agency contact that transcends the client's contact with any individual social worker. The case record also implements the agency's accountability to the community. It provides a permanent, documented account of services to clients. The interviewer about to record the interview faces the essential question, what should be recorded and how should the recording be organized? Just as purpose guides interview interaction, so it guides selection of material for recording. Traditionally, social work recording has been designed to meet a number of different purposes. We record to achieve more effective practice, to provide material for in-service training and teaching, and for research purposes. There is no consensus on the principal purpose of social work recording. Consequently, recording has served these various purposes with limited effectiveness, and has served no one purpose well.

11. According to the above passage, the relationship between recording and interviewing costs for social work purposes is such that

    A. recording is *three times* more expensive than interviewing
    B. recording is *one-third* as expensive as interviewing
    C. recording is *four times* more expensive than interviewing
    D. interviewing is *much more* expensive than recording

12. The *one* of the following that is SPECIFICALLY mentioned as a purpose of case recording is

    A. saving time   B. economy
    C. research   D. convenience

13. Of the following, according to the passage, a MAJOR contributing factor to the expense of case recording is

    A. supervision   B. in-service training
    C. research   D. record reading time

14. It can be concluded that the author's opinion regarding the capacity of social work recording to achieve its various purposes is

    A. enthusiastic   B. guarded   C. neutral   D. confused

Questions 15-17.

DIRECTIONS: Answer Questions 15 through 17 based SOLELY on the information contained in the following passage.

On the State level, in an effort to obtain better administration and delivery of services in the Medicaid program, the Governor has appointed a committee to advise the State Commissioner of Social Welfare on medical care services. Included on this committee are representatives of the medical, dental, pharmaceutical, nursing, and social work professions, as well as persons representing the fields of mental health, home health agencies, nursing homes, schools of health science, public health and welfare administrations, and the general public. Several of the committee members are physicians in private practice who represent and uphold the interests of the private physicians who care for Medicaid patients.

The committee not only makes recommendations on the standards, quality and costs of medical services, personnel, and facilities, but also helps identify unmet needs, and assists in long-range planning, evaluation and utilization of services. It advises, as requested, on administrative and fiscal matters, and also interprets the programs and goals to professional groups.

On the City level, representatives of the county medical societies of New York City meet periodically with Medicaid administrators to discuss problems and consider proposals. It is hoped that the county medical societies will assume the responsibility of informing citizens as to where they can receive medical care under Medicaid.

15. Based on information in the above passage, it can be inferred that the group on the advisory committee likely to be LEAST objective in their recommendations would be the representatives of the

    A. public health and welfare administrations
    B. general public
    C. private physicians
    D. schools of health science

16. The above passage suggests that a problem with the Medicaid program in New York City is that

    A. the Mayor has not appointed a committee to work with the City Commissioner of Social Services
    B. many people do not know where they can go to obtain medical care under the program
    C. the county medical societies of New York City do not meet often enough with the Medicaid program administrators
    D. citizens do not take the initiative to seek out sources of available medical care under the program

17. According to the above passage, the Governor's objective in appointing the advisory committee was to

    A. obtain more cooperation from the New York City county medical societies
    B. get the members of the committee to provide medical care services to Medicaid recipients
    C. help improve the Medicaid program in all its aspects, including administration and provision of services
    D. persuade a greater number of private physicians and other health care professionals to accept Medicaid patients

18. Which one of the following is the MOST desirable method of recording an interview with a client?

    A. Record sufficient detail to provide the reader with an understanding of the client's situation and needs
    B. Record as much detail as possible to minimize the necessity of relying on memory later
    C. Quote the key points made by the client to avoid potential misunderstanding and embarrassment
    D. Take very few notes and record as much as you can remember upon completion of the interview

19. Assume that you are preparing to write a case summary giving the essential information pertaining to the facts of a case clearly and briefly. Of the following, the MOST appropriate form to use for recording this type of information would be a

    A. process record   B. discharge planning report
    C. case folder   D. face sheet

20. The one of the following records which would be MOST useful in helping to develop a treatment plan for a patient is the

    A. face sheet
    B. medical service order
    C. social service medical record
    D. psycho-social summary

KEY (CORRECT ANSWERS)

1.	D	11.	A
2.	A	12.	C
3.	C	13.	D
4.	C	14.	B
5.	C	15.	C
6.	C	16.	B
7.	B	17.	C
8.	B	18.	A
9.	A	19.	D
10.	A	20.	D

EXAMINATION SECTION
TEST 1

DIRECTIONS: Each question or incomplete statement is followed by several suggested answers or completions. Select the one that BEST answers the question or completes the statement. *PRINT THE LETTER OF THE CORRECT ANSWER IN THE SPACE AT THE RIGHT.*

1. An interview is BEST conducted in private primarily because 1.____
   A. the person interviewed will tend to be less self-conscious
   B. the interviewer will be able to maintain his continuity of thought better
   C. it will insure that the interview is "off the record"
   D. people tend to "show off" before an audience

2. An interviewer can BEST establish a good relationship with the person being interviewed by 2.____
   A. assuming casual interest in the statements made by the person being interviewed
   B. taking the point of view of the person interviewed
   C. controlling the interview to a major extent
   D. showing a genuine interest in the person

3. An interviewer will be better able to understand the person interviewed and his problems if he recognizes that much of the person's behavior is due to motives 3.____
   A. which are deliberate   B. of which he is unaware
   C. which are inexplicable   D. which are kept under control

4. An interviewer's attention must be directed toward himself as well as toward the person interviewed. 4.____
   This statement means that the interviewer should
   A. keep in mind the extent to which his own prejudices may influence his judgment
   B. rationalize the statements made by the person interviewed
   C. gain the respect and confidence of the person interviewed
   D. avoid being too impersonal

5. More complete expression will be obtained from a person being interviewed if the interviewer can create the impression that 5.____
   A. the data secured will become part of a permanent record
   B. official information must be accurate in every detail
   C. it is the duty of the person interviewed to give accurate data
   D. the person interviewed is participating in a discussion of his own problems

6. The practice of asking leading questions should be avoided in an interview because the
    A. interviewer risks revealing his attitudes to the person being interviewed
    B. interviewer may be led to ignore the objective attitudes of the person interviewed
    C. answers may be unwarrantedly influenced
    D. person interviewed will resent the attempt to lead him and will be less cooperative

7. A good technique for the interviewer to use in an effort to secure reliable data and to reduce the possibility of misunderstanding is to
    A. use casual undirected conversation, enabling the person being interviewed to talk about himself, and thus secure the desired information
    B. adopt the procedure of using direct questions regularly
    C. extract the desired information from the person being interviewed by putting him on the defensive
    D. explain to the person being interviewed the information desired and the reason for needing it

8. You are interviewing a patient to determine whether she is eligible for medical assistance. Of the many questions that you have to ask her, some are routine questions that patients tend to answer willingly and easily. Other questions are more personal and some patients tend to resent being asked them and avoid answering them directly.
    For you to begin the interview with the more personal questions would be
    A. *desirable*, because the end of the interview will go smoothly and the patient will be left with a warm feeling
    B. *undesirable*, because the patient might not know the answers to the questions
    C. *desirable*, because you will be able to return to these questions later to verify the accuracy of the responses
    D. *undesirable*, because you might antagonize the patient before you have had a chance to establish rapport

9. While interviewing a patient about her family composition, the patient asks you whether you are married.
    Of the following, the MOST appropriate way for you to handle this situation is to
    A. answer the question briefly and redirect her back to the topic under discussion
    B. refrain from answering the question and proceed with the interview
    C. advise the patient that it is more important that she answer your questions than that you answer hers, and proceed with the interview
    D. promise the patient that you will answer her question later, in the hope that she will forget, and redirect her back to the topic under discussion

10. In response to a question about his employment history, a patient you are interviewing rambles and talks about unrelated matters.
    Of the following, the MOST appropriate course of action for you to take FIRST is to

A. ask questions to direct the patient back to his employment history
B. advise him to concentrate on your questions and not to discuss irrelevant information
C. ask him why he is resisting a discussion of his employment history
D. advise him that if you cannot get the information you need, he will not be eligible for medical assistance

11. Suppose that a person you are interviewing becomes angry at some of the questions you have asked, calls you meddlesome and nosy, and states that she will not answer those questions.
Of the following, which is the BEST action for you to take?
    A. Explain the reasons the questions are asked and the importance of the answers
    B. Inform the interviewee that you are only doing your job and advise her that she should answer your questions or leave the office
    C. Report to your supervisor what the interviewee called you and refuse to continue the interview
    D. End the interview and tell the interviewee she will not be serviced by your department

12. Suppose that during the course of an interview the interviewee demands in a very rude way that she be permitted to talk to your supervisor or someone in charge.
Which of the following is probably the BEST way to handle this situation?
    A. Inform your supervisor of the demand and ask her to speak to the interviewee
    B. Pay no attention to the demands of the interviewee and continue the interview
    C. Report to your supervisor and tell her to get another interviewer for this interviewee
    D. Tell her you are the one "in charge" and that she should talk to you

13. Of the following, the outcome of an interview by an aide depends MOST heavily on the
    A. personality of the interviewee
    B. personality of the aide
    C. subject matter of the questions asked
    D. interaction between aide and interviewee

14. Some patients being interviewed are primarily interested in making a favorable impression.
The aide should be aware of the fact that such patients are more likely than other patients to
    A. try to anticipate the answers the interviewer is looking for
    B. answer all questions openly and frankly
    C. try to assume the role of interviewer
    D. be anxious to get the interview over as quickly as possible

15. The type of interview which an aide usually conducts is substantially different from most interviewing situations in all of the following aspects EXCEPT the
    A. setting
    B. kinds of clients
    C. techniques employed
    D. kinds of problems

16. During an interview, an aide uses a "leading question."
This type of question is so-called because it generally
    A. starts a series of questions about one topic
    B. suggests the answer which the aide wants
    C. forms the basis for a following "trick" question
    D. sets, at the beginning, the tone of the interview

17. Casework interviewing is always directed to the client and his situation.
The one of the following which is the MOST accurate statement with respect to the proper focus of an interview is that the
    A. caseworker limits the client to concentration on objective data
    B. client is generally permitted to talk about facts and feelings with no direction from the caseworker
    C. main focus in casework interviews is on feelings rather than facts
    D. caseworker is responsible for helping the client focus on any material which seems to be related to his problems or difficulties

18. Assume that you are conducting a training program for the caseworkers under your supervision. At one of the sessions, you discuss the problem of interviewing a dull and stupid client who gives a slow and disconnected case history.
The BEST of the following interviewing methods for you to recommend in such a case in order to ascertain facts is for the caseworker to
    A. ask the client leading questions requiring "yes" or "no" answers
    B. request the client to limit his narration to the essential facts so that the interview can be kept as brief as possible
    C. review the story with the client, patiently asking simple questions
    D. tell the client that unless he is more cooperative he cannot be helped to solve his problem

19. A recent development in casework interviewing procedure, known as multiple-client interviewing, consists of interviews of the entire family at the same time. However, this may not be an effective casework method in certain situations.
Of the following, the situation in which the standard individual interview would be preferable is when
    A. family member derive consistent and major gratification from assisting each other in their destructive responses
    B. there is a crucial family conflict to which the members are reacting
    C. the family is overwhelmed by interpersonal anxieties which have not been explored
    D. the worker wants to determine the pattern of family interaction to further his diagnostic understanding

20. A follow-up interview was arranged for an applicant in order that he could furnish 20.____
certain requested evidence. At this follow-up interview, the applicant still fails
to furnish the necessary evidence.
It would be MOST advisable for you to
   A. advise the applicant that he is now considered ineligible
   B. ask the applicant how soon he can get the necessary evidence and set a date for another interview
   C. question the applicant carefully and thoroughly to determine if he has misrepresented or falsified any information
   D. set a date for another interview and tell the applicant to get the necessary evidence by that time

KEY (CORRECT ANSWERS)

1.	A	11.	A
2.	D	12.	A
3.	B	13.	D
4.	A	14.	A
5.	D	15.	C
6.	C	16.	B
7.	D	17.	D
8.	D	18.	C
9.	A	19.	A
10.	A	20.	B

TEST 2

DIRECTIONS: Each question or incomplete statement is followed by several suggested answers or completions. Select the one that BEST answers the question or completes the statement. *PRINT THE LETTER OF THE CORRECT ANSWER IN THE SPACE AT THE RIGHT.*

1. In interviewing, the practice of anticipating an applicant's answers to questions is generally
    A. *desirable*, because it is effective and economical when it is necessary to interview large numbers of applicants
    B. *desirable*, because many applicants have language difficulties
    C. *undesirable*, because it is the inalienable right of every person to answer as he sees fit
    D. *undesirable*, because applicants may tend to agree with the answer proposed by the interviewer even when the answer is not entirely correct

    1.____

2. When an initial interview is being conducted, one way of starting is to explain the purpose of the interview to the applicant.
   The practice of starting the interview with such an explanation is generally
    A. *desirable*, because the applicant can then understand why the interview is necessary and what will be accomplished by it
    B. *desirable*, because it creates the rapport which is necessary to successful interviewing
    C. *undesirable*, because time will be saved by starting directly with the questions which must be asked
    D. *undesirable*, because the interviewer should have the choice of starting an interview in any manner he prefers

    2.____

3. For you to use responses such as "That's interesting," "Uh-huh," and "Good" during an interview with a patient is
    A. *desirable*, because they indicate that the investigator is attentive
    B. *undesirable*, because they are meaningless to the patient
    C. *desirable*, because the investigator is not supposed to talk excessively
    D. *undesirable*, because they tend to encourage the patient to speak freely

    3.____

4. During the course of a routine interview, the BEST tone of voice for an interviewer to use is
    A. authoritative   B. uncertain
    C. formal   D. conversational

    4.____

5. It is recommended that interviews which inquire into the personal background of an individual should be held in private.
   The BEST reason for this practice is that privacy
    A. allows the individual to talk freely about the details of his background
    B. induces contemplative thought on the part of the interviewed individual
    C. prevents any interruptions by departmental personnel during the interview
    D. most closely resembles the atmosphere of the individual's personal life

    5.____

2 (#2)

6. Assume that you are interviewing a patient to determine whether he has any savings accounts.
   To obtain this information, the MOST effective way to phrase your question would be:
   A. "You don't have any savings, do you?"
   B. "At which bank do you have a savings account?"
   C. "Do you have a savings account?"
   D. "May I assume that you have a savings account?"

7. You are interviewing a patient who is not cooperating to the extent necessary to get all required information. Therefore, you decide to be more forceful in your approach.
   In this situation, such a course of action is
   A. *advisable*, because such a change in approach may help to increase the patient's participation
   B. *advisable*, because you will be using your authority more effectively
   C. *inadvisable*, because you will not be able to change this approach if it doesn't produce results
   D. *inadvisable*, because an aggressive approach generally reduces the validity of the interview

8. You have attempted to interview a patient on two separate occasions, and both attempts were unsuccessful. The patient has been totally uncooperative and you sense a personal hostility toward you.
   Of the following, the BEST way to handle this type of situation would be to
   A. speak to the patient in a courteous manner and ask him to explain exactly what he dislikes about you
   B. inform the patient that you will not allow personality conflicts to disrupt the interview
   C. make no further attempt to interview the patient and recommend that he be billed in full
   D. discuss the problem with your supervisor and suggest that another investigator be assigned to try to interview the patient

9. At the beginning of an interview, a patient with normal vision tells you that he is reluctant to discuss his finances. You realize that it will be necessary in this case to ask detailed questions about his net income.
   When you begin this line of questioning, of the following, the LEAST important aspect you should consider is your
   A. precise wording of the question   B. manner of questioning
   C. tone of voice   D. facial expressions

10. A caseworker under your supervision has been assigned the task of interviewing a man who is applying for foster home placement for his two children. The caseworker seeks your advice as to how to question this man, stating that she finds the applicant to be a timid and self-conscious person who seems torn between the necessity of having to answer the worker's questions truthfully and the effect he thinks his answers will have on his application.

Of the following, the BEST method for the caseworker to use in order to determine the essential facts in this case is to
- A. assure the applicant that he need not worry since the majority of applications for foster home placement are approved
- B. delay the applicant's narration of the facts important to the case until his embarrassment and fears have been overcome
- C. ignore the statements made by the applicant and obtain all the required information from his friends and relatives
- D. inform the applicant that all statements made by him will be verified and are subject to the law governing perjury

11. Assume that a worker is interviewing a boy in his assigned group in order to help him find a job.
   At the BEGINNING of the interview, the worker should
   - A. suggest a possible job for the youth
   - B. refer the youth to an employment agency
   - C. discuss the youth's work history and skills with him
   - D. refer the youth to the manpower and career development agency

12. As part of the investigation to locate an absent father, you make a field visit to interview one of the father's friends. Before beginning the interview, you identify yourself to the friend and show him your official identification.
   For you to do this is, generally,
   - A. *good practice*, because the friend will have proof that you are authorized to make such confidential investigations
   - B. *poor practice*, because the friend may not answer your questions when he knows why you are interviewing him
   - C. *good practice*, because your supervisor can confirm from the friend that you actually made the interview
   - D. *poor practice*, because the friend may warn the absent father that your agency is looking for him

13. You are interviewing a client in his home as part of your investigation of an anonymous complaint that he has been receiving Medicaid fraudulently. During the interview, the client frequently interrupts your questions to discuss the hardships of his life and the bitterness he feels about his medical condition.
   Of the following, the BEST way for you to deal with these discussions is to
   - A. cut them off abruptly, since the client is probably just trying to avoid answering your questions
   - B. listen patiently, since these discussions may be helpful to the client and may give you information for your investigation
   - C. remind the client that you are investigating a complaint against him and he must answer directly
   - D. seek to gain the client's confidence by discussing any personal or medical problems which you yourself may have

14. While interviewing an absent father to determine his ability to pay child support, you realize that his answers to some of your questions contradict his answers to other questions.
    Of the following, the BEST way for you to try to get accurate information from the father is to
    A. confront him with his contradictory answers and demand an explanation from him
    B. use your best judgment as to which of his answers are accurate and question him accordingly
    C. tell him that he has misunderstood your questions and that he must clarify his answers
    D. ask him the same questions in different words and follow up his answer with related questions

15. Assume that an applicant, obviously under a great deal of stress, talks continuously and rambles, making it difficult for you to determine the exact problem and her need.
    In order to make the interview more successful, it would be BEST for you to
    A. interrupt the applicant and ask her specific questions in order to get the information you need
    B. tell the applicant that her rambling may be a basic cause of her problem
    C. let the applicant continue talking as long as she wishes
    D. ask the applicant to get to the point because other people are waiting for you

16. A worker must be able to interview clients all day and still be able to listen and maintain interest.
    Of the following, it is MOST important for you to show interest in the client because, if you appear interested,
    A. the client is more likely to appreciate your professional status
    B. the client is more likely to disclose a greater amount of information
    C. the client is less likely to tell lie
    D. you are more likely to gain your supervisor's approval

17. When you are interviewing clients, it is important to notice and record how they say what they say—angrily, nervously, or with "body English"—because these signs may
    A. tell you that the client's words are the opposite of what the client feels and you may need to dig to find out what those feeling are
    B. be the prelude to violent behavior which no aide is prepared to handle
    C. show that the client does not really deserve serious consideration
    D. be important later should you be asked to defend what you did for the client

18. The patient you are interviewing is reticent and guarded in responding to your questions. He is not providing the information needed to complete his application for medical assistance.
    In this situation, the one of the following which is the MOST appropriate course of action for you to take FIRST is to

A. end the interview and ask him to contact you when he is ready to answer your questions
B. advise the patient that you cannot end the interview until he has provided all the information you need to complete the application
C. emphasize to the patient the importance of the questions and the need to answer them in order to complete the application
D. advise the patient that if he answers your questions the interview will be easier for both of you

19. At the end of an interview with a patient, he describes a problem he is having with his teenage son, who is often truant and may be using narcotics. The patient asks you for advice in handling his son.
Of the following, the MOST appropriate action for you to take is to
   A. make an appointment to see the patient and his son together
   B. give the patient a list of drug counseling programs to which he may refer his son
   C. suggest to the patient that his immediate concern should be his own hospitalization rather than his son's problem
   D. tell the patient that you are not qualified to assist him but will attempt to find out who can

19.____

20. A MOST appropriate condition in the use of direct questions to obtain personal data in an interview is that, whenever possible,
   A. the direct questions be used only as a means of encouraging the person interviewed to talk about himself
   B. provision be made for recording the information
   C. the direct questions be used only after all other methods have failed
   D. the person being interviewed understands the reason for requesting the information

20.____

KEY (CORRECT ANSWERS)

1.	D	11.	C
2.	A	12.	A
3.	A	13.	B
4.	D	14.	D
5.	A	15.	A
6.	B	16.	B
7.	A	17.	A
8.	D	18.	C
9.	A	19.	D
10.	B	20.	D

READING COMPREHENSION
UNDERSTANDING AND INTERPRETING WRITTEN MATERIAL
EXAMINATION SECTION
TEST 1

DIRECTIONS: Each question or incomplete statement is followed by several suggested answers or completions. Select the one that BEST answers the question or completes the statement. *PRINT THE LETTER OF THE CORRECT ANSWER IN THE SPACE AT THE RIGHT.*

Questions 1-5.

DIRECTIONS: Questions 1 through 5 are to be answered SOLELY on the basis of the following paragraph.

    In counting the poor, the Social Security Administration has developed two poverty thresholds that <u>designate</u> families as either *poor* or *near poor*. The Administration assumed that the poor would spend the same proportion of income on food as the rest of the population but that, obviously, since their income was smaller, their range of selection would be narrower. In the Low Cost Food Plan, the amount <u>allocated to</u> food from the average expenditure was cut to the minimum that the Agriculture Department said could still provide American families with an adequate diet. This Low Cost Food Plan was used to characterize the *near poor* category, and an even lower Economy Food Plan was used to characterize the *poor* category. The Economy Food Plan was based on $7.00 a person for food each day, assuming that all food would be prepared at home. The Agriculture Department estimates that only about 10 percent of persons spending $7.00 or less for food each day actually were able to get a nutritionally adequate diet.

1. Of the following, the MOST suitable title for the above paragraph would be 1.____
    A. THE SUPERIORITY OF THE ECONOMY PLAN OVER THE LOW COST PLAN
    B. THE NEED FOR A NUTRITIONALLY ADEQUATE DIET
    C. FOOD EXPENDITURES OF THE POOR AND THE NEAR POOR
    D. DIET IN THE UNITED STATES

2. According to the above paragraph, the Social Security Administration assumed, in setting its poverty levels, that the poor 2.____
    A. spend a smaller proportion of income for food than the average non-poor
    B. would not eat in restaurants
    C. as a group includes only those with a nutritionally inadequate diet
    D. spend more money on food than the near poor

3. According to the above paragraph, it would be CORRECT to state that the Low Cost Food Plan
   A. is above the minimum set by the Agriculture Department for a nutritionally adequate diet
   B. gives most people a nutritionally inadequate diet
   C. is lower than the Economy Food Plan
   D. represents the amount spent by the near poor

4. As estimated by the Department of Agriculture, the percentage of people spending $7.00 or less a day for food who did NOT get a nutritionally adequate diet was
   A. 100%   B. 90%   C. 10%   D. 0%

5. As used in the above paragraph, the underlined words allocated to mean MOST NEARLY
   A. offered for
   B. assigned to
   C. wasted on
   D. spent on

Questions 6-11.

DIRECTIONS: Questions 6 through 11 are to be answered SOLELY on the basis of the information given in the paragraph below.

Three years ago, the City introduced a program of reduced transit rates for the elderly. It was hoped that this program would increase the travel of the elderly and help them maintain a greater measure of independence. About 600,000 of the 800,000 eligible residents are currently enrolled in the program. To be eligible, a person must be 65 years of age or older and not employed full-time. Riding for reduced fare is permitted between 10:00 A.M. and 4:00 P.M. and between 7:00 P.M. and Midnight on weekdays, and 24 hours a day on Saturdays, Sundays, and holidays.

In a City university study, based on a sampling of 728 enrollees interviewed, it was learned that 51 percent are able to travel more and 30.8 percent had been able to save enough money to make a noticeable difference in their budgets as a result of the reduced-fare program.

It has been recommended that reduced-fare programs be extended to encourage the use of transit lines in off hours by other groups such as the poor, the very young, housewives, and the physically handicapped. To implement this recommendation, it would be necessary for the Federal government to increase transit subsidies.

6. Which one of the following titles would be the BEST for the above passage?
   A. A PROGRAM OF REDUCED TRANSIT RATES FOR THE ELDERLY
   B. RECOMMENDATIONS FOR EXTENDING PROGRAMS FOR THE ELDERLY
   C. CITY UNIVERSITY STUDY ON THE RELATIONSHIP OF AGE AND TRAVEL
   D. ELIGIBILITY REQUIREMENTS FOR THE REDUCED RATE PROGRAM

3 (#1)

7. Approximately what percentage of the eligible residents is currently enrolled in the reduced-fare program?
   A. 25%   B. 50%   C. 65%   D. 75%

7.____

8. Which one of the following persons is NOT eligible for the reduced-fare program? A
   A. woman, age 67, employed part-time as a stenographer
   B. handicapped man, age 62
   C. blind man, age 66, employed part-time as a transcribing typist
   D. housewife, age 70

8.____

9. At which one of the following times would the reduced-fare NOT be permitted for an eligible elderly person?
   A. Sunday, 6:00 P.M.
   B. Christmas Day, 2:00 A.M.
   C. Tuesday, 9:00 A.M.
   D. Thursday, 8:00 P.M.

9.____

10. Of the 728 enrollees interviewed in the City university study of the reduced-fare program, it was found that
    A. the majority traveled more and saved money at the same time
    B. more than half traveled less and, therefore, saved money
    C. about half traveled more and about one-third saved money
    D. the majority saved money but traveled the same rate as before

10.____

11. According to the above passage, what would be necessary to extend the reduced-fare program to other groups of people?
    A. Increasing the eligible age to 68
    B. Reducing the hours when half-fare is permitted
    C. Increasing the fare for other riders
    D. Increasing the transit subsidies by the Federal government

11.____

Questions 12-14.

DIRECTIONS: Questions 12 through 14 are to be answered SOLELY on the basis of the following passage.

Local public welfare agencies, in general, recognize that more time is required for Aid to Dependent Children cases and General Assistance cases than for Old Age Assistance cases, and that the intensive work required in Child Welfare Service cases necessitates special planning with regard to limiting caseloads for workers to prevent their carrying too large a number of cases. A General Assistance case often includes several persons, while Old Age Assistance cases are on an individual basis. Although the average cost of a case per month has continued to increase for all assistance programs, these programs have retained their relative cost positions. The average monthly cost of a case has been lowest for Aid to the Aged, followed, in ascending order, by Aid to the Blind, Aid to Dependent Children, and General Assistance, with the cost per case of the last mentioned program averaging more than four times that for Aid to the Aged. On the other hand, the proportion of Aid to the Aged cases is rising while the percentage of General Assistance cases is declining.

12. Some types of cases require more time or more intensive work than others. 12.____
The one of the following statements which MOST accurately illustrates this point, according to the above paragraph, is:
    A. Aid to the Blind cases often included several persons and, therefore, are very time-consuming, while Old Age Assistance cases require intensive casework
    B. Aid to Dependent Children cases often involve complicated situations and, therefore, require intensive casework, while Aid to the Blind cases are extremely time-consuming
    C. Old Age Assistance cases are relatively less time-consuming, while Child Welfare Service cases entail detailed casework
    D. Old Age Assistance cases are time-consuming, while General Assistance cases are comparatively simple

13. If a public welfare official were to set up several caseloads, with each caseload 13.____
containing the same total number of cases but with a varying number in each of the different types of assistance, the caseload which would MOST likely require the GREATEST expenditure of time would be the one with a majority of
    A. Aid to the Blind cases and Aid to Dependent Children cases
    B. General Assistance cases and Aid to Dependent Children cases
    C. Old Age Assistance cases and Aid to the Blind cases
    D. Old Age Assistance cases and General Assistance cases

14. According to the above paragraph, the one of the following statements which 14.____
is the MOST accurate with regard to the cost of welfare services is that
    A. the average monthly cost for each Aid to Dependent Children case was higher than for each Aid to the Blind case but lower than for each Aid to the Aged case
    B. the cost per case for General Assistance has risen four times as fast as the cost per case for Aid to the Aged
    C. there has been a decrease in the proportion of General Assistance cases, but the cost per case in this category has increased
    D. more than four times as much money was spent in total for all the cases in the General Assistance program than for those in the Aid to the Aged program

Questions 15-17.

DIRECTIONS: Questions 15 through 17 are to be answered SOLELY on the basis of the following passage.

Aid to dependent children shall be given to a parent or other relative as herein specified for the benefit of a child or children under sixteen years of age or of a minor or minors between sixteen and eighteen years of age if in the judgment of the administrative agency: (1) the granting of an allowance will be in the interest of such child or minor, and (2) the parent or other relative is a fit person to bring up such child or minor so that his physical, mental, and moral well-being will be safeguarded, and (3) aid is necessary to enable such parent or other relative to do so, and (4) such child or minor is a resident of the state on the date of application for aid, and (5) such minor between sixteen and eighteen years of age is regularly attending school in accordance with the regulations of the department. An allowance may be granted for the aid of such child or minor who has been deprived of parental support or care by reason of the death, continued absence from the home, or physical or mental incapacity of a parent, and who is living with his father, mother, grandfather, grandmother, brother, sister, stepfather, stepmother, stepbrother, stepsister, uncle, or aunt. In making such allowances, consideration shall be given to the ability of the relative making application and of any other relatives to support and are for or to contribute to the support and care of such child or minor. In making all such allowances, it shall be made certain that the religious faith of the child or minor shall be preserved and protected.

15. The above passage is concerned PRIMARILY with
    A. the financial ability of persons applying for public assistance
    B. compliance on the part of applicants with the *settlement* provisions of the law
    C. the fitness of parents or other relatives to bring up physically, mentally, or morally delinquent children between the ages of sixteen and eighteen
    D. eligibility for aid to dependent children

16. On the basis of the above passage, the MOST accurate of the following statements is:
    A. Mary Doe, mother of John, age 18, is entitled to aid for her son if he is attending school regularly
    B. Evelyn Stowe, mother of Eleanor, age 13, is not entitled to aid for Eleanor if she uses her home for immoral purposes
    C. Ann Roe, cousin of Helen, age 14, is entitled to aid for Helen if the latter is living with her
    D. Peter Moe, uncle of Henry, age 15, is not entitled to aid for Henry if the latter is living with him

17. The above passage is PROBABLY an excerpt of the
    A. Administrative Code   B. Social Welfare Law
    C. Federal Security Act   D. City Charter

Questions 18-20.

DIRECTIONS: Questions 18 through 20 are to be answered SOLELY on the basis of the information contained in the following passage.

On the state level, in an effort to obtain better administration and delivery of services in the Medicaid program, the Governor has appointed a committee to advise the State Commissioner of Social Welfare on medical care services. Included on this committee are representatives of the medical, dental, pharmaceutical, nursing, and social work professions, as well as persons representing the fields of mental health, home health agencies, nursing homes, schools of health science, public health and welfare administrations, and the general public. Several of the committee members are physicians in private practice who represent and uphold the interests of the private physicians who care for Medicaid patients.

The committee not only makes recommendations on the standards, quality, and costs of medical services, personnel, and facilities, but also helps identify unmet needs, and assists in long-range planning, evaluation, and utilization of services. It advises, as requested, on administrative and fiscal matters, and also interprets the programs and goals to professional groups.

On the city level, representatives of the county medical societies of the city meet periodically with Medicaid administrators to discuss problems and consider proposals. It is hoped that the county medical societies will assume the responsibility of informing citizens as to where they can receive medical care under Medicaid.

18. Based on information in the above passage, it can be inferred that the group on the advisory committee likely to be LEAST objective in their recommendations would be the representatives of the
    A. public health and welfare administrations
    B. general public
    C. private physicians
    D. schools of health science

19. The above passage suggests that a problem with the Medicaid program is that
    A. the Mayor has not appointed a committee to work with the City Commissioner of Social Services
    B. many people do not know where they can go to obtain medical care under the program
    C. the county medical societies do not meet often enough with the Medicaid program administrators
    D. citizens do not take the initiative to seek out sources of available medical care under the program

20. According to the above passage, the Governor's objective in appointing the advisory committee was to
    A. obtain more cooperation from the county medical societies
    B. get the members of the committee to provide medical care services to Medicaid recipients
    C. help improve the Medicaid program in all its aspects, including administration and provision of services
    D. persuade a greater number of private physicians and other health care professionals to accept Medicaid patients

Questions 21-25.

DIRECTIONS: Questions 21 through 25 are to be answered SOLELY on the basis of the following passage.

Any person who is living in the city and is otherwise eligible may be granted public assistance whether or not he has state residence. However, since the city does not contribute to the cost of assistance granted to persons who are without state residence, the cases of all recipients must be formally identified as to whether or not each member of the household has state residence.

To acquire state residence, a person must have resided in the state continuously for one year. Such residence is not lost unless the person is out of the state continuously for a period of one year or longer. Continuous residence does not include any period during which the individual is a patient in a hospital, an inmate of a public institution or of an incorporated private institution, a resident on a military reservation or a minor residing in a boarding home while under the care of an authorized agency. Receipt of public assistance does not prevent a person from acquiring state residence. State residence, once acquired, is not lost because of absence from the state while a person is serving in the United States Armed Forces or the Merchant Marine; nor does a member of the family of such a person lose state residence while living with or near that person in these circumstances.

Each person, regardless of age, acquires or loses state residence as an individual. There is no derivative state residence except for an infant at the time of birth. He is deemed to have state residence if he is in the custody of both parents and either one of them has state residence, or if the parent having custody of his has state residence.

21. According to the above passage, an infant is deemed to have state residence at the time of his birth if
    A. he is born in the state but neither of his parents is a resident
    B. he is in the custody of only one parent, who is not a resident but his other parent is a resident
    C. his brother and sister are residents
    D. he is in the custody of both his parents but only one of them is a resident

22. The Jones family consists of five members. Jack and Mary Jones have lived in New York State continuously for the past eighteen months after having lived in Ohio since they were born. Of their three children, one was born ten months ago and has been in the custody of his parents since birth. Their second child lived in Ohio until six months ago and then moved in with his parents. Their third child had never lived in New York until he moved with his parents to New York eighteen months ago. However, he entered the Armed Forces one month later and has not lived in New York since that time. Based on the above passage, how many members of the Jones family are New York State residents?
    A. 2   B. 3   C. 4   D. 5

23. Assuming that each of the following individuals has lived continuously in the state for the past year, and has never previously lived in the state, which one of them is a state resident?
    A. Jack Salinas, who has been an inmate in a state correctional facility for six months of the year
    B. Fran Johnson, who has lived on an Army base for the entire year
    C. Arlene Snyder, who married a non-resident during the past year
    D. Gary Phillips, who was a patient in a Veterans Administration Hospital for the entire year

24. The above passage implies that the reason for determining whether or not a recipient of public assistance is a state resident is that
    A. the cost of assistance for non-residents is not a city responsibility
    B. non-residents living in the city are not eligible for public assistance
    C. recipients of public assistance are barred from acquiring state residence
    D. the city is responsible for the full cost of assistance to recipients who are residents

25. Assume that the Rollins household in the city consists of six members at the present time – Anne Rollins, her three children, her aunt, and her uncle. Anne Rollins and one of her children moved to the city seven months ago. Neither of them had previously lived in the state. Her other two children have lived in the city continuously for the past two years, as has her aunt. Anne Rollins' uncle had lived in the city continuously for many years until two years ago. He then entered the Armed Forces and has returned to the city within the past month. Based on the above passage, how many members of the Rollins' household are state residents?
    A. 2   B. 3   C. 4   D. 6

KEY (CORRECT ANSWERS)

1.	C	11.	D
2.	B	12.	C
3.	D	13.	B
4.	B	14.	C
5.	B	15.	D
6.	A	16.	B
7.	D	17.	B
8.	B	18.	C
9.	C	19.	B
10.	C	20.	C

21.	D
22.	B
23.	C
24.	A
25.	C

TEST 2

DIRECTIONS: Each question or incomplete statement is followed by several suggested answers or completions. Select the one that BEST answers the question or completes the statement. *PRINT THE LETTER OF THE CORRECT ANSWER IN THE SPACE AT THE RIGHT.*

Questions 1-4.

DIRECTIONS: Questions 1 through 4 are to be answered SOLELY on the basis of the following passage.

The loss of control over the use of a drug — called addiction where there is both physical and psychological dependence, and habituation where there is psychological dependence without physical dependence — is, regardless of the particular drug involved, a disease. Both chronic alcoholism and narcotics addiction are usually recognized as diseases.

It is inappropriate to invoke the criminal process against persons who have lost control over the use of dangerous drugs solely because these persons are drug users. Once a person has lost control over his use of drugs, the existence of offenses such as drug use or simple possession will not deter his use. Having lost control, he cannot choose to conform his conduct to the requirements of the law by refraining from use. He is non-deterrable.

Admittedly, there may be times before a person loses control over his use of drugs when he did have a choice of whether to use or not to use, or to stop using. Because of this, punishing him for use or simple possession would not offend the principle that to be punishable conduct must be a result of free choice.

1. Of the following, the MOST suitable title for the above passage is   1.____
   A. DRUG ADDICTION
   B. DRUG ABUSE AND PUNISHMENT
   C. HABITUATION AND THE CRIMINAL PROCESS
   D. PREVENTING DRUG-RELATED CRIME

2. According to the above passage, addiction and habituation are   2.____
   A. identical in meaning because both are diseases related to drug use
   B. identical in meaning because both involve dependence on drugs
   C. similar to the extent that both involve physical dependence on a drug
   D. similar to the extent that both involve psychological dependence on a drug

3. According to the above passage, punishing drug abusers would be justifiable ONLY if their behavior were   3.____
   A. elective   B. non-deterrable
   C. chronic   D. dangerous

4. According to the above passage, punishing a person for simple possession of drugs is
   A. appropriate under certain circumstances
   B. inappropriate because the person could not have acted otherwise
   C. necessary for the protection of society
   D. unfair because it penalizes past conduct

Questions 5-8.

DIRECTIONS: Questions 5 through 8 are to be answered SOLELY on the basis of the following passage.

The usually explanation for drunken behavior is that alcohol, which is a physiological depressant, impairs reasoning and inhibition powers before it depresses the ability to act and to express emotion.

The purely physiological effects of alcohol are very much like of those of fatigue. Individual personality and social and cultural influences apparently greatly determine how these effects are reflected in changed behavior as alcohol is consumed. Therefore, one can assert that alcohol alone does not cause drunken behavior; rather, drunken behavior expresses personal character, cultural traditions, and social circumstances, as they influence a person's reactions to the physiological effects of alcohol on his body.

For some people, and in some circumstances, these personal, cultural, and social factors may readily express themselves as criminal behavior. The most obvious case, of course, is public drunkenness.

The exact relationship between various crimes and various stages of intoxication is not completely known. G.M. Scott believes that the moderate stages of intoxication are the ones usually associated with crime since the latter states of intoxication make performance of crime impossible. Dr. Banay found that many drunks are drawn into crime not only by the need of money to replace wages that drinking prevents them from earning, but also by their increased irritability and pugnacity. He discovered that most of the sex offenses for which offenders are committed to state prisons show a relation between alcohol and the crime and that the average sex case is a clear-cut illustration of the hypothesis that alcohol covers up an underlying condition and that some dormant tendency is either brought to the surface or aggravated by alcohol.

In addition to drunken behavior resulting in criminal acts, it is also connected to several other important social problems. Reference can be made particularly to dependency, unemployment, desertion, divorce, vagrancy, and suicide. For all of these social ills, alcohol acts as the physiological depressing agent which influences one's deviation from normative behavior.

5. Discussions of intoxication customarily state that alcohol
   A. initially affects the analytic faculty
   B. initially affects the ability to express feelings
   C. reduces the desire for money
   D. stimulates perception of the true nature of one's condition

6. Which one of the following hypotheses would Dr. Banay MOST likely support?
   A. The casual drinker is LESS likely to commit a crime than the chronic drinker.
   B. An aggressive drunk is LIKELY to have aggressive tendencies when not under the influence of alcohol.
   C. The UNDERLYING cause of most sex offenses is excessive drinking.
   D. There is NO connection between cultural background and drunken behavior.

7. The title BEST suited for the above passage is
   A. HOW ALCOHOL INFLUENCES POTENTIAL SEXUAL OFFENDERS
   B. STAGES OF INTOXICATION
   C. THE ROLE OF ALCOHOLIC CONSUMPTION IN HUMAN BEHAVIOR
   D. THE RELATIONSHIP BETWEEN ALCOHOL AND EMOTION

8. The writer implies that
   A. a desire to destroy oneself is a frequent side effect of drinking intoxicating liquors
   B. a person who is drunk may find it easier to kill himself
   C. there is a pattern of drinking behavior in the background of most suicides
   D. there is no relationship between the problems of drinking and suicide

Questions 9-11.

DIRECTIONS: Questions 9 through 11 are to be answered SOLELY on the basis of the following paragraph.

A substantial source of opposition to legalizing heroin is those people who are convinced that this idea is simply another form of social and economic injustice. Instead of getting at the fundamental causes of addiction, they say, the result will be to turn hundreds of young addicts into the living dead.

9. According to the above paragraph, opposition to legalizing heroin is based, in part, on the belief that
   A. some addicts will become walking dead people
   B. the problem is entirely one of educating individuals
   C. the pushers will simply turn to other criminal activities
   D. the root causes of addiction are still mysterious

10. Which of the following treatment approaches would the author of the above paragraph be MOST likely to oppose?
    A. Ambulatory detoxification   B. Methadone maintenance
    C. Drug-free therapeutic community   D. Youth intervention program

11. As used in the above paragraph, the underlined word substantial means MOST NEARLY
    A. known   B. large   C. strange   D. unanimous

Questions 12-16.

DIRECTIONS: Questions 12 through 16 are to be answered SOLELY on the basis of the following paragraph.

In the last dozen years or so, there has <u>emerged</u> an argument which obviously has a certain persuasiveness among young people: that drugs are being used, not as an expression of antisocial behavior or for escape, but to define a different, anti-establishment culture. Drugs can, of course, be used that way; it's very possible to have a youth culture that uses drugs as a <u>norm</u>. But it's also possible to have a youth culture that is opposed to using drugs as a <u>norm</u>. For example, in China, around 1910, a very effective campaign against opium was led largely by students who felt that the use of drugs was the reason China had suffered so much at the hands of the Western powers.

12. According to the above paragraph, the Chinese students opposed the use of opium because
    A. it contradicted Chinese religious values
    B. it interfered with their studies
    C. they believed it weakened their country
    D. the Western powers encouraged addiction

13. The writer of the above paragraph seems to believe that there is no necessary connection between
    A. escapism and culture
    B. norms and values
    C. students and politics
    D. youth and drugs

14. According to the above paragraph, it is possible to have a youth culture that considers the use of drugs
    A. completely acceptable
    B. legally defensible
    C. morally uplifting
    D. physically beneficial

15. The underlined word <u>emerged</u> means MOST NEARLY
    A. come into view
    B. gone through
    C. required to be
    D. responded quickly

16. As used in the above paragraph, the underlined word <u>norm</u> means MOST NEARLY
    A. argument of explanation
    B. error or mistake
    C. pleasure or reward
    D. rule or average

Questions 17-20.

DIRECTIONS: Questions 17 through 20 are to be answered SOLELY on the basis of the following paragraph.

Alcoholics are to be found in both sexes, in every major religious and racial group, and at all socio-economic levels. What they share in common are psychiatric problems which they seek to ease or dull through alcohol. Ideally, every heavy drinker should be subjected to intensive psychiatric therapy. Unfortunately, even psychiatric treatment is not always successful, and in any case the nation has allocated neither the funds nor the personnel nor the facilities that would be required for such a massive therapeutic effort.

17. According to the above paragraph, national priorities in connection with psychiatric treatment for alcoholism do NOT provide for
    A. fair and impartial treatment
    B. large-scale programs
    C. proper religious values
    D. strict laws against alcoholism

18. According to the above paragraph, alcoholics are MOST likely to be
    A. emotionally disturbed
    B. ultimately curable
    C. unable to function
    D. under medical care

19. As used in the above paragraph, the underlined word intensive means MOST NEARLY
    A. concentrated   B. modern   C. prompt   D. specialized

20. As used in the above paragraph, the underlined word allocated means MOST NEARLY
    A. assigned   B. conserved   C. desired   D. recognized

Questions 21-25.

DIRECTIONS: Questions 21 through 25 are to be answered SOLELY on the basis of the following paragraph.

The practice of occasionally adulterating marijuana complicates analysis of the effects of marijuana use in non-controlled settings. Behavioral changes which are attributed to marijuana may actually derive from the adulterants or from the interaction of tetrahydrocannabinols and adulterants. Similarly, in today's society, marijuana is often used simultaneously or sequentially with other psycho-active drugs. When drug interactions occur, the simultaneous presence of two or more drugs in the body can exert effects which are more than that which would result from the simple addition of the effects of each drug used separately. Thus, the total behavioral response may be greater than the sum of its parts. For example, if a given dose of marijuana induced two units of perceptual distortion, and a certain dose of LSD given alone induced two units of perceptual distortion, the simultaneous administration of these doses of marijuana and LSD may induce not four but five units of perceptual distortion.

6 (#2)

21. According to the above paragraph, the concurrent presence of two drugs in the body can 21.____
    A. compound the effects of both drugs
    B. reduce perceptual distortion
    C. simulate psychotic symptoms
    D. be highly toxic

22. Based on the above paragraph, it is MOST reasonable to assume that tetrahydrocannabinols are 22.____
    A. habit-forming substances
    B. components of marijuana
    C. similar to quinine or milk-sugar
    D. used as adulterants

23. Based on the above paragraph, it is MOSTS reasonable to state that marijuana is 23.____
    A. most affected by adulterants when used as a psycho-active drug
    B. erroneously considered to be less harmful than other drugs
    C. frequently used in connection with other mind-affecting drugs
    D. occasionally used as an adjunct to LSD in order to reduce bad reactions

24. As used in the above paragraph, the underlined word attributed means MOST NEARLY 24.____
    A. originally unsuspected
    B. identical in action
    C. known as a reason
    D. ascribed by way of cause

25. As used in the above paragraph, the underlined word induced means MOST NEARLY 25.____
    A. caused   B. projected   C. required   D. displayed

KEY (CORRECT ANSWERS)

1.	B		11.	B
2.	D		12.	C
3.	A		13.	D
4.	A		14.	A
5.	A		15.	A
6.	B		16.	D
7.	C		17.	B
8.	B		18.	A
9.	A		19.	A
10.	B		20.	A

21. A
22. B
23. C
24. D
25. A

PREPARING WRITTEN MATERIALS
EXAMINATION SECTION
TEST 1

DIRECTIONS: Each question consists of a sentence which may be classified appropriately under one of the following four categories:
A. Incorrect because of faulty grammar or sentence structure.
B. Incorrect because of faulty punctuation.
C. Incorrect because of faulty spelling or capitalization.
D. Correct

Examine each sentence carefully. Then, in the space at the right, print the capital letter preceding the option which is the BEST of the four suggested above. All incorrect sentences contain only one type of error. Consider a sentence correct if it contains none of the types of errors mentioned, although there may be other correct ways of expressing the same thought.

1. The fire apparently started in the storeroom, which is usually locked. 1._____

2. On approaching the victim two bruises were noticed by this officer. 2._____

3. The officer, who was there examined the report with great care. 3._____

4. Each employee in the office had a separate desk. 4._____

5. The suggested procedure is similar to the one now in use. 5._____

6. No one was more pleased with the new procedure than the chauffeur. 6._____

7. He tried to pursuade her to change the procedure. 7._____

8. The total of the expenses charged to petty cash were high. 8._____

9. An understanding between him and I was finally reached. 9._____

10. It was at the supervisor's request that the clerk agreed to postpone his vacation. 10._____

11. We do not believe that it is necessary for both he and the clerk to attend the conference. 11._____

12. All employees, who display perseverance, will be given adequate recognition. 12._____

13. He regrets that some of us employees are dissatisfied with our new assignments. 13._____

14. "Do you think that the raise was merited," asked the supervisor?   14.____

15. The new manual of procedure is a valuable supplament to our rules and   15.____
    regulation.

16. The typist admitted that she had attempted to pursuade the other employees   16.____
    to assist her in her work.

17. The supervisor asked that all amendments to the regulations be handled by   17.____
    you and I.

18. They told both he and I that the prisoner had escaped.   18.____

19. Any superior officer, who, disregards the just complaints of his subordinates,   19.____
    is remiss in the performance of his duty.

20. Only those members of the national organization who resided in the Middle   20.____
    west attended the conference in Chicago.

21. We told him to give the investigation assignment to whoever was available.   21.____

22. Please do not disappoint and embarass us by not appearing in court.   22.____

23. Despite the efforts of the Supervising mechanic, the elevator could not be   23.____
    started.

24. The U.S. Weather Bureau, weather record for the accident date was checked.   24.____

KEY (CORRECT ANSWERS)

1.	D	11.	A
2.	A	12.	B
3.	B	13.	D
4.	D	14.	B
5.	D	15.	C
6.	D	16.	C
7.	C	17.	A
8.	A	18.	A
9.	A	19.	B
10.	D	20.	C

21.	D
22.	C
23.	C
24.	B

TEST 2

DIRECTIONS: Each question consists of a sentence. Some of the sentences contain errors in English grammar or usage, punctuation, spelling, or capitalization. A sentence does not contain an error simply because it could be written in a different manner. Choose answer:
- A. If the sentence contains an error in English grammar or usage.
- B. if the sentence contains an error in punctuation.
- C. If the sentence contains an error in spelling or capitalization
- D. If the sentence does not contain any errors.

1. The severity of the sentence prescribed by contemporary statutes—including both the former and the revised New York Penal Laws—do not depend on what crime was intended by the offender.   1.____

2. It is generally recognized that two defects in the early law of attempt played a part in the birth of burglary: (1) immunity from prosecution for conduct short of the last act before completion of the crime, and (2) the relatively minor penalty imposed for an attempt (it being a common law misdemeanor) vis-à-vis the completed offense.   2.____

3. The first sentence of the statute is applicable to employees who enter their place of employment, invited guests, and all other persons who have an express or implied license or privilege to enter the premises.   3.____

4. Contemporary criminal codes in the United States generally divide burglary into various degrees, differentiating the categories according to place, time and other attendent circumstances.   4.____

5. The assignment was completed in record time but the payroll for it has not yet been prepaid.   5.____

6. The operator, on the other hand, is willing to learn me how to use the mimeograph.   6.____

7. She is the prettiest of the three sisters.   7.____

8. She doesn't know; if the mail has arrived.   8.____

9. The doorknob of the office door is broke.   9.____

10. Although the department's supply of scratch pads and stationery have diminished considerably, the allotment for our division has not been reduced.   10.____

11. You have not told us whom you wish to designate as your secretary.   11.____

12. Upon reading the minutes of the last meeting, the new proposal was taken up for consideration.   12.____

13. Before beginning the discussion, we locked the door as a precautionery measure.   13.____

14. The supervisor remarked, "Only those clerks, who perform routine work, are permitted to take a rest period."   14.____

15. Not only will this duplicating machine make accurate copies, but it will also produce a quantity of work equal to fifteen transcribing typists.   15.____

16. "Mr. Jones," said the supervisor, "we regret our inability to grant you an extention of your leave of absence."   16.____

17. Although the employees find the work monotonous and fatigueing, they rarely complain.   17.____

18. We completed the tabulation of the receipts on time despite the fact that Miss Smith our fastest operator was absent for over a week.   18.____

19. The reaction of the employees who attended the meeting, as well as the reaction of those who did not attend, indicates clearly that the schedule is satisfactory to everyone concerned.   19.____

20. Of the two employees, the one in our office is the most efficient.   20.____

21. No one can apply or even understand, the new rules and regulations.   21.____

22. A large amount of supplies were stored in the empty office.   22.____

23. If an employee is occassionally asked to work overtime, he should do so willingly.   23.____

24. It is true that the new procedures are difficult to use but, we are certain that you will learn them quickly.   24.____

25. The office manager said that he did not know who would be given a large allotment under the new plan.   25.____

KEY (CORRECT ANSWERS)

1.	A	11.	D
2.	D	12.	A
3.	D	13.	C
4.	C	14.	B
5.	C	15.	A
6.	A	16.	C
7.	D	17.	C
8.	B	18.	B
9.	A	19.	D
10.	A	20.	A

21. B
22. A
23. C
24. B
25. D

TEST 3

DIRECTIONS: Each of the following sentences may be classified MOST appropriately under one of the following categories:
- A. Faulty because of incorrect grammar
- B. Faulty because of incorrect punctuation
- C. Faulty because of incorrect capitalization
- D. Correct

Examine each sentence carefully. Then, in the space at the right, print the capital letter preceding the option which is the BEST of the four suggested above. All incorrect sentence contain but one type of error. Consider a sentence correct if it contains none of the types of errors mentioned, even though there may be other correct ways of expressing the same thought.

1. The desk, as well as the chairs, were moved out of the office.   1._____

2. The clerk whose production was greatest for the month won a day's vacation as first prize.   2._____

3. Upon entering the room, the employees were found hard at work at their desks.   3._____

4. John Smith our new employee always arrives at work on time.   4._____

5. Punish whoever is guilty of stealing the money.   5._____

6. Intelligent and persistent effort lead to success no matter what the job may be.   6._____

7. The secretary asked, "can you call again at three o'clock?"   7._____

8. He told us, that if the report was not accepted at the next meeting, it would have to be rewritten.   8._____

9. He would not have sent the letter if he had known that it would cause so much excitement.   9._____

10. We all looked forward to him coming to visit us.   10._____

11. If you find that you are unable to complete the assignment please notify me as soon as possible.   11._____

12. Every girl in the office went home on time but me; there was still some work for me to finish.   12._____

13. He wanted to know who the letter was addressed to, Mr. Brown or Mr. Smith.   13._____

14. "Mr. Jones, he said, please answer this letter as soon as possible."   14._____

15. The new clerk had an unusual accent inasmuch as he was born and educated in the south. 15._____

16. Although he is younger than her, he earns a higher salary. 16._____

17. Neither of the two administrators are going to attend the conference being held in Washington, D.C. 17._____

18. Since Miss Smith and Miss Jones have more experience than us, they have been given more responsible duties. 18._____

19. Mr. Shaw the supervisor of the stock room maintains an inventory of stationery and office supplies. 19._____

20. Inasmuch as this matter affects both you and I, we should take joint action. 20._____

21. Who do you think will be able to perform this highly technical work? 21._____

22. Of the two employees, John is considered the most competent. 22._____

23. He is not coming home on tuesday; we expect him next week. 23._____

24. Stenographers, as well as typists must be able to type rapidly and accurately. 24._____

25. Having been placed in the safe we were sure that the money would not be stolen. 25._____

KEY (CORRECT ANSWERS)

1.	A	11.	B
2.	D	12.	D
3.	A	13.	A
4.	B	14.	B
5.	D	15.	C
6.	A	16.	A
7.	C	17.	A
8.	B	18.	A
9.	D	19.	B
10.	A	20.	A

21. D
22. A
23. C
24. B
25. A

TEST 4

DIRECTIONS: Each of the following sentences consist of four sentences lettered A, B, C, and D. One of the sentences in each group contains an error in grammar or punctuation. Indicate the INCORRECT sentence in each group. *PRINT THE LETTER OF THE CORRECT ANSWER IN THE SPACE AT THE RIGHT.*

1. A. Give the message to whoever is on duty.
   B. The teacher who's pupil won first prize presented the award.
   C. Between you and me, I don't expect the program to succeed.
   D. His running to catch the bus caused the accident.

   1.____

2. A. The process, which was patented only last year is already obsolete.
   B. His interest in science (which continues to the present) led him to convert his basement into a laboratory.
   C. He described the book as "verbose, repetitious, and bombastic".
   D. Our new director will need to possess three qualities: vision, patience, and fortitude.

   2.____

3. A. The length of ladder trucks varies considerably.
   B. The probationary fireman reported to the officer to who he was assigned.
   C. The lecturer emphasized the need for we firemen to be punctual.
   D. Neither the officers nor the members of the company knew about the new procedure.

   3.____

4. A. Ham and eggs is the specialty of the house.
   B. He is one of the students who are on probation.
   C. Do you think that either one of us have a chance to be nominated for president of the class?
   D. I assume that either he was to be in charge or you were.

   4.____

5. A. Its a long road that has no turn.
   B. To run is more tiring than to walk.
   C. We have been assigned three new reports: namely, the statistical summary, the narrative summary, and the budgetary summary.
   D. Had the first payment been made in January, the second would be due in April.

   5.____

6. A. Each employer has his own responsibilities.
   B. If a person speaks correctly, they make a good impression.
   C. Every one of the operators has had her vacation.
   D. Has anybody filed his report?

   6.____

7. A. The manager, with all his salesmen, was obliged to go.
   B. Who besides them is to sign the agreement?
   C. One report without the others is incomplete.
   D. Several clerks, as well as the proprietor, was injured.

   7.____

2 (#4)

8. A. A suspension of these activities is expected. 8.____
    B. The machine is economical because first cost and upkeep are low.
    C. A knowledge of stenography and filing are required for this position.
    D. The condition in which the goods were received shows that the packing was not done properly.

9. A. There seems to be a great many reasons for disagreement. 9.____
    B. It does not seem possible that they could have failed.
    C. Have there always been too few applicants for these positions?
    D. There is no excuse for these errors.

10. A. We shall be pleased to answer your question. 10.____
    B. Shall we plan the meeting for Saturday?
    C. I will call you promptly at seven.
    D. Can I borrow your book after you have read it?

11. A. You are as capable as I. 11.____
    B. Everyone is willing to sign but him and me.
    C. As for he and his assistant, I cannot praise them too highly.
    D. Between you and me, I think he will be dismissed.

12. A. Our competitors bid above us last week. 12.____
    B. The survey which was began last year has not yet been completed.
    C. The operators had shown that they understood their instructions.
    D. We have never ridden over worse roads.

13. A. Who did they say was responsible? 13.____
    B. Whom did you suspect?
    C. Who do you suppose it was?
    D. Whom do you mean?

14. A. Of the two propositions, this is the worse. 14.____
    B. Which report do you consider the best—the one in January or the one in July?
    C. I believe this is the most practicable of the many plans submitted.
    D. He is the youngest employee in the organization.

15. A. The firm had but three orders last week. 15.____
    B. That doesn't really seem possible.
    C. After twenty years scarcely none of the old business remains.
    D. Has he done nothing about it?

KEY (CORRECT ANSWERS)

1.	B	6.	B	11.	C
2.	A	7.	D	12.	B
3.	C	8.	C	13.	A
4.	C	9.	A	14.	B
5.	A	10.	D	15.	C

PREPARING WRITTEN MATERIAL

PARAGRAPH REARRANGEMENT
COMMENTARY

The sentences that follow are in scrambled order. You are to rearrange them in proper order and indicate the letter choice containing the correct answer at the space at the right.

Each group of sentences in this section is actually a paragraph presented in scrambled order. Each sentence in the group has a place in that paragraph; no sentence is to be left out. You are to read each group of sentences and decide upon the best order in which to put the sentences so as to form a well-organized paragraph.

The questions in this section measure the ability to solve a problem when all the facts relevant to its solution are not given.

More specifically, certain positions of responsibility and authority require the employee to discover connection between events sometimes, apparently, unrelated. In order to do this, the employee will find it necessary to correctly infer that unspecified events have probably occurred or are likely to occur. This ability becomes especially important when action must be taken on incomplete information.

Accordingly, these questions require competitors to choose among several suggested alternatives, each of which presents a different sequential arrangement of the events. Competitors must choose the MOST logical of the suggested sequences.

In order to do so, they may be required to draw on general knowledge to infer missing concepts or events that are essential to sequencing the given events. Competitors should be careful to infer only what is essential to the sequence. The plausibility of the wrong alternatives will always require the inclusion of unlikely events or of additional chains of events which are NOT essential to sequencing the given events.

It's very important to remember that you are looking for the best of the four possible choices, and that the best choice of all may not even be one of the answers you're given to choose from.

There is no one right way to solve these problems. Many people have found it helpful to first write out the order of the sentences, as they would have arranged them, on their scrap paper before looking at the possible answers. If their optimum answer is there, this can save them some time. If it isn't, this method can still give insight into solving the problem. Others find it most helpful to just go through each of the possible choices, contrasting each as they go along. You should use whatever method feels comfortable and works for you.

While most of these types of questions are not that difficult, we've added a higher percentage of the difficult type, just to give you more practice. Usually there are only one or two questions on this section that contain such subtle distinctions that you're unable to answer confidently. And you then may find yourself stuck deciding between two possible choices, neither of which you're sure about.

EXAMINATION SECTION
TEST 1

DIRECTIONS: Each group of sentences in this section is actually a paragraph presented in scrambled order. Each sentence in the group has a place in that paragraph; no sentence is to be left out. You are to read each group of sentences, so as to form a well-organized paragraph. Before trying to answer the questions which follow each group of sentences, jot down the correct order of the sentences. Then answer each of the questions by printing the letter of the correct answer in the space at the right. Remember that you will receive credit only for answers marked.

P. The infant only feels the positive stimulation of warmth and food and does not differentiate the warmth and food from their source, mother.
Q. The infant, at the moment of birth, would feel the fear of dying if gracious fate did not preserve it from any awareness of the anxiety involved in the separation from mother.
R. The infant's state, then, is what has been called narcissism.
S. Mother is warmth, mother is food, mother is the euphoric state of satisfaction and security.
T. Even after being born, the infant is not yet aware of itself, and of the world as being outside of itself.

1. Which sentence did you put before Sentence Q?

   A. P
   B. R
   C. S
   D. T
   E. None of the above. Sentence Q is first.

2. Which sentence did you put after Sentence S?

   A. P
   B. Q
   C. R
   D. T
   E. None of the above. Sentence S is last.

3. Which sentence did you put before Sentence P?

   A. Q
   B. R
   C. S
   D. T
   E. None of the above. Sentence P is first.

4. Which sentence did you put after Sentence P?

   A. Q
   B. R
   C. S
   D. T
   E. None of the above. Sentence P is last.

5. Which sentence did you put after Sentence R?

   A. P
   B. Q
   C. S
   D. T
   E. None of the above. Sentence R is last.

KEY (CORRECT ANSWERS)

1. E
2. C
3. D
4. C
5. E

1. C
2. E
3. B
4. A
5. A

KEY (CORRECT ANSWERS)

1. A
2. E
3. B
4. D
5. C

TEST 3

DIRECTIONS: Each group of sentences in this section is actually a paragraph presented in scrambled order. Each sentence in the group has a place in that paragraph; no sentence is to be left out. You are to read each group of sentences, so as to form a well-organized paragraph. Before trying to answer the questions which follow each group of sentences, jot down the correct order of the sentences. Then answer each of the questions by printing the letter of the correct answer in the space at the right. Remember that you will receive credit only for answers marked.

P. Indeed, in his time, Freud's theories of sex had a challenging and revolutionary character.
Q. Sexual mores have changed so much that Freud's theories no longer are shocking to the middle classes.
R. Freud has been criticized for his overevaluation of sex.
S. But what was true sixty years ago is no longer true.
T. This criticism resulted from a wish to remove an element from Freud's system which might arouse criticism among conventionally-minded people.

1. Which sentence did you put last?
   A. P   B. Q   C. R   D. S   E. T

2. Which sentence did you put before Sentence Q?
   A. P
   B. R
   C. S
   D. T
   E. None of the above. Sentence Q is first.

3. Which sentence did you put after Sentence T?
   A. P
   B. Q
   C. R
   D. S
   E. None of the above. Sentence T is last.

4. Which sentence did you put before Sentence R?
   A. P
   B. Q
   C. S
   D. T
   E. None of the above. Sentence R is first.

5. Which sentence did you put after Sentence R?
   A. P
   B. Q
   C. S
   D. T
   E. None of the above. Sentence R is last.

KEY (CORRECT ANSWERS)

1. B
2. C
3. A
4. E
5. D

TEST 4

DIRECTIONS: Each group of sentences in this section is actually a paragraph presented in scrambled order. Each sentence in the group has a place in that paragraph; no sentence is to be left out. You are to read each group of sentences, so as to form a well-organized paragraph. Before trying to answer the questions which follow each group of sentences, jot down the correct order of the sentences. Then answer each of the questions by printing the letter of the correct answer in the space at the right. Remember that you will receive credit only for answers marked.

P. Early Scandanavian accounts, as well, are too mythological and legendary to serve as history.
Q. The first trustworthy written evidence of a kingdom of Denmark belongs to the beginning of the Viking period.
R. Ancient Roman knowledge of this remote country was fragmentary and unreliable.
S. Archaeology and the study of place names, however, provide a certain amount of information about the earliest settlements.
T. Everything before that is prehistory.

1. Which sentence did you put fourth?
   A. P   B. B. Q   C. C. R   D. D. S   E. E. T

2. Which sentence did you put after Sentence T?
   A. Q
   B. R
   C. S
   D. None of the above. Sentence T is last.

3. Which sentence did you put after Sentence Q?
   A. P
   B. R
   C. S
   D. T
   E. None of the above. Sentence Q is last.

4. Which sentence did you put before Sentence Q?
   A. P
   B. R
   C. S
   D. T
   E. None of the above. Sentence Q is first.

5. Which sentence did you put after Sentence P?
   A. Q
   B. R
   C. S
   D. T
   E. None of the above. Sentence P is last.

KEY (CORRECT ANSWERS)

1. A
2. C
3. D
4. E
5. C

TEST 5

DIRECTIONS: Each group of sentences in this section is actually a paragraph presented in scrambled order. Each sentence in the group has a place in that paragraph; no sentence is to be left out. You are to read each group of sentences, so as to form a well-organized paragraph. Before trying to answer the questions which follow each group of sentences, jot down the correct order of the sentences. Then answer each of the questions by printing the letter of the correct answer in the space at the right. Remember that you will receive credit only for answers marked.

P. In 1268, ambassadors were required to surrender all gifts they had received on their missions.
Q. In the 13th century, the Venetian republic began to lay down rules of conduct for its ambassadors.
R. In 1288, it was decreed that ambassadors were to report in writing on the results of their missions.
S. Such reports are a mine of historical material.
T. It is in Venice that the origins of modern diplomacy are to be sought.

1. Which sentence did you put second?
   A. P   B. Q   C. R   D. S   E. T

2. Which sentence did you put after Sentence R?
   A. P
   B. Q
   C. S
   D. T
   E. None of the above. Sentence R is last.

3. Which sentence did you put before Sentence P?
   A. Q
   B. R
   C. S
   D. T
   E. None of the above. Sentence P is first.

4. Which sentence did you put before Sentence T?
   A. P
   B. Q
   C. R
   D. S
   E. None of the above. Sentence T is first.

5. Which sentence did you put last?
   A. P   B. B. Q   C. C. R   D. D. S   E. E. T

KEY (CORRECT ANSWERS)

1. B
2. C
3. A
4. E
5. D

www.ingramcontent.com/pod-product-compliance
Lightning Source LLC
Chambersburg PA
CBHW082210300426
44117CB00016B/2743